The Art of Reasoning

An Interactive Introduction to Traditional Logic

by

Michael W. Tkacz

and

George H. Watson, S.J.

KENDALL/HUNT PUBLISHING COMPANY
4050 Westmark Drive   Dubuque, Iowa 52002

In Memoriam

John A. Oesterle

Dialectici eruditissimi

Preface to the First Edition

This book is a modest contribution to a long tradition of logic textbooks which began with the Greeks of late antiquity and includes such notable modern works as Antoine Arnauld's Port Royal <u>Logic</u> and Lewis Carroll's <u>Symbolic Logic</u>. It concerns what is commonly called traditional logic. It must, however, be said from the start that only a portion of traditional logic is treated here. The intention is to provide the student with a quick and practical means to develop the skills of recognizing traditional argument forms and detecting certain common informal fallacies. This, of course, is hardly the whole of traditional logic. Important topics, such as definition and division, are not included. Others, such as induction, are treated only briefly. Even where a form of argument is treated at some length, consideration is limited. Analysis of categorical syllogisms, for example, is limited to Venn diagrams. The traditional rules for validity as well as the method of reduction are omitted.

This means that the book may not be suitable for all logic courses, but it is hoped that it might fill the need for a brief introduction to certain elements of traditional logic as a preparation for the study of philosophy. Thus, this book might best be used as the initial part of an introductory course in philosophy or in a short intersession or summer course. Though there are many fine logic and critical thinking textbooks available, this book may serve those who do not need or have the time for a more detailed and elaborate treatment.

The interactive approach taken in this book demands that the student make immediate application of what is learned. This, after all, is the best way to develop a skill. The material is presented in 20 sections each of which is accompanied by a series of exercises which the student must complete if the material is to be mastered. Additional exercises, including short self-testing exercises, are included at the end of the book for those who wish supplementary practice material. In many of these exercises, arguments are presented in the natural context of conversation. It is hoped that this will provide a more practical and interesting way for the student to learn the material.

I am grateful for the technical assistance of Laurie Bergheim and Sandra Hank of the Gonzaga University Faculty Services staff. Thanks are also due to my wife, Dr. Catherine Brown Tkacz, who generously read through the whole text and made many valuable suggestions. Perhaps my greatest debt is owed to the many generations of logicians who, from Aristotle on, developed and transmitted the art of reasoning. It is to the memory of one of the best of these logicians, Professor John A. Oesterle, that this book is dedicated.

Michael W. Tkacz
Gonzaga University

Preface to the Second Edition

For the second edition of this text we have made numerous corrections and introduced clarifications where necessary. Exercises which experience has shown to be unsuccessful have been rewritten. A treatment of the distinction between universal particularization and universal generalization has been added. Rather than add this material to the sections on the proposition at the beginning of the text, it has been appended to the treatment of fallacies of generalization (see Exercise 29). This material, however, has been written in such a way that the instructor who wishes to treat this distinction along with the material on the proposition can easily do so.

The purpose of the book remains the same as in the first edition: to provide a quick and practical means for students to develop the basic skills of traditional logic as a preparation for the study of philosophy. Thus, the treatment of various forms of deductive and inductive argument and of fallacies remains brief. Instructors who wish to provide their students with a more extensive introduction to one or another of the topics treated will find that additional material can be easily incorporated into a course based on this text.

We wish to thank our colleague, Dr. Douglas Kries, for his insightful review of these materials and his many valuable suggestions. We are also grateful to Sandra Hank of the Gonzaga University Faculty Services staff for her technical assistance.

Michael W. Tkacz
Gonzaga University

George H. Watson, S.J.
Seattle University

Table of Contents

Table of Contents (continued)

§1 Giving Reasons

Everyone has beliefs. Some beliefs are profound: God exists; for every action there is an equal and opposite reaction; honesty is the best policy. Some beliefs are common: whole milk tastes better than low-fat milk; I left my car keys in the kitchen; Carol prefers to sit in the front of the class. Whether they are profound or common, beliefs are about what is true or false of the real world.

It is always possible that a person has a belief which he thinks is true when it is really false. The ancient Greek philosopher Aristotle believed that the earth does not move. This, of course, is false. An astronomer of our own day believes that the earth is in motion on its own axis and in orbit around the sun. Both Aristotle and the modern astronomer are concerned that their beliefs be true. After all, what is the point of holding a false belief knowing it to be false? Everyone wants his beliefs to be true. Still, beliefs may be false.

The possibility of false belief is why somebody's belief might be challenged. One person's belief may be questioned by another person who holds a different belief on the same subject. In this case, the person whose belief is being questioned will either have to defend his belief or abandon it. It is also possible that we might question our own beliefs. We may wonder whether what we believe to be true really is true and, so, we may challenge ourselves. Again, we have two choices: we must either defend our belief to ourselves or we must abandon our belief.

Usually we will not simply abandon our beliefs when they are challenged. After all, we hold the belief because we think that it is true. This leaves the other alternative: we must defend our belief, either to ourselves or to others. We do this by giving reasons for our belief. A reason is another belief which we claim leads us to the belief which is being questioned. Usually this other belief is one which we also think is true and often one which the challenger thinks is true also. We then claim that, if you accept this other belief, then you must also accept the belief being challenged as well.

Suppose that two people agree that the earth casts a curved shadow on the surface of the moon during an eclipse and that anything which casts a curved shadow must be round. One of these people might then claim that believing these two things gives one a good reason to believe that the earth is round. In other words, accepting as true the first two beliefs leads one to accept as true the belief that the earth is round.

This process of giving reasons for the truth of our beliefs is called argument. Argument is a tool we can use to help assure us that our beliefs about the real world are true.

Every argument has at least two parts. The part which expresses the belief being defended is called the conclusion. The part or parts expressing the reasons supporting the truth of the conclusion are called the premises. The conclusion is the reason why the argument exists. The person who gives an argument in support of a conclusion does so because he wants to show that the conclusion is true. The premises, on the other hand, exist in the argument for the sake of the conclusion. If the arguer were not interested in the truth of the conclusion, then he would not express the premises.

In order to understand how an argument provides reasons for a conclusion, it is necessary that one be able to distinguish the conclusion from the premises. If a person is unable to do this, then that person cannot tell which belief is being defended and which beliefs are being given as reasons for the beliefs being defended. The following passages each express an argument. Read each carefully and write out the conclusion and the premises.

1.   Every student of Master Giles is from Germany and all Germans drink beer. It must be true, then, that every student of Master Giles drinks beer.

        conclusion: _____

        first premise: _____

        second premise: _____

2.   It must be true that the ancient philosophers were wise. Anyone whose books are still studied after so many centuries is greatly respected and anyone who is so greatly respected is wise.

        conclusion: _____

        first premise: _____

        second premise: _____

3.	If this student of Master Giles is from Germany, then he speaks German. This student is one of Master Giles' students and is from Germany. Therefore, he must speak German.

conclusion: _____

first premise: _____

second premise: _____

4.	Brother John must be in the library. The reason I think this is true is that Brother Joseph told me he saw him there and Brother Joseph always speaks the truth.

conclusion: _____

first premise: _____

second premise: _____

5.	I have just learned that all of Master Giles' students failed the logic examination. Thus, there are students of Master Giles who failed the logic examination.

conclusion: _____

premise: _____

6.	None of Brother John's manuscripts are easy to read, because his handwriting is so poor.

conclusion: _____

premise: _____

You may have noticed in Exercise 1 that there are certain English words and phrases which tend to go with conclusions or with premises. We can use our knowledge of these words and phrases to help us pick out conclusions and premises.

Conclusions are often introduced by such **conclusion indicators** as "therefore," "thus," "so," "it follows that," "hence," "we can conclude that," "then," "we have shown that," and many others. Premises are often introduced by such **premises indicators** as "for," "because," "since," "the reason is that," and many others. Some of these words are almost always used as conclusion or premise indicators. (For example, "therefore" is almost always used in arguments to introduce a conclusion.) Some of these words, however, have other uses not connected with argumentation. (For example, "then" is sometimes used to indicate temporal sequence.) So, we must be careful not to assume that we have a conclusion or a premise simply because of the presence of a conclusion or premise indicator. A good rule to follow when reading is to ask yourself whether the author is giving reasons for a belief. If so, then the author is arguing and there must be a conclusion. If not, then check to see whether the indicator word or phrase is being used in some non-argumentative way. It is also important to notice that it is possible to express a conclusion or a premise without any indicator word or phrase at all. Again, a good practice when reading is to ask yourself whether the author is giving reasons in support of some belief and, if so, what is the belief he is trying to support or prove.

The fact that some premise and conclusion indicators are often used in ways that have nothing to do with argument shows that language is not always used to express arguments. It is important that we be able to determine when the passage we are reading contains an argument and when it does not. Read the following passages and determine which contain arguments and which do not. For those passages which do contain arguments, underline the conclusion.

1. At the request of his monks, Abbot Anselm explained what he had written by saying we know that there are many good things. Each of these goods are either good through themselves or good through something else. All goods cannot be good through themselves, because then there would be nothing by which we rightly say that they are good. Therefore, they must be good through some one good thing which is goodness itself. That which is supremely good in this way we call God.

   Does this passage contain an argument? Yes ___ No ___

2. Anselm was a simple monk for many years before being elected abbot. He originally came from Lombardy and, having decided to dedicate his life to good works and the study of the sacred scriptures entered the monastery at Bec in Normandy. His intellectual talents were much admired at Bec and after some time he was appointed prior. It was during this period that he wrote many of his most learned treatises, including the book in which he gave his famous proof for the existence of God.

    Does this passage contain an argument? Yes ___ No ___

3. It is sometimes claimed that Anselm came to Bec after 1060. This, however, cannot be correct because, according to his medieval biographer Eadmer, Anselm was a student of Lanfranc from this time on and Lanfranc was abbot at Bec during this period.

    Does this passage contain an argument? Yes ___ No ___

4. Brother Anselm first studied the basic arts at Bec including the art of logic, which the ancients called "dialectics." He then began his study of the sacred scriptures and of the holy fathers, especially the most learned writings of Augustine who was bishop of Hippo Regius in Africa many years ago.

    Does this passage contain an argument? Yes ___ No ___

5. Anselm set out to use his mortal intellect to understand the teachings of the Christian faith. The most basic of these teachings is the existence of God. Beginning with the idea of a perfect being, Anselm says that human beings can have in their minds the idea of an absolutely perfect being. The name we give to the perfect being is "God." Now, perfection implies existence. Hence God exists.

    Does this passage contain an argument? Yes ___ No ___

§2 Being Consistent

The reason why it is possible that any belief can be challenged is that, for every belief there is another possible belief which is incompatible with it. Another way of saying this is that the fact that any given belief is true makes some other belief false. Consider, for example, the following:

[1] The earth is a sphere.

[2] The earth is a cube.

Both of these sentences express possible beliefs. If somebody holds [1] to be true, then he will probably hold [2] to be false. This is because [1] and [2] cannot be true together. Since we know that whatever is a sphere cannot be a cube at the same time, we know that believing that [2] is true amounts to believing that the following is true:

[3] The earth is not a sphere.

It is impossible that both [1] and [3] be true at the same time. This is the case for any belief whatsoever, no matter what it is about. Any belief which contradicts a belief we know to be true must be false and any belief which contradicts a belief we know to be false must be true. [1] and [3] express contradictory beliefs.

If we wish our beliefs to be true, then we cannot allow that it is possible that contradictory beliefs are true at the same time. To allow that this is possible is to tolerate inconsistency in our beliefs. If we allow inconsistency in our beliefs, then at least some of our beliefs will be false. If this happens, then our beliefs will be unreliable guides to the way the world really is.

Being consistent in our beliefs is not just an academic exercise. It is, in fact, our way of dealing with the real world. This can be easily seen if we call to mind that our beliefs are the basis for our plans and our actions. If our beliefs are inconsistent, then we will not be able to act on the basis of them. If our plans are inconsistent, at least some of our plans will be frustrated. Of course, being wrong about what really is and being frustrated in our plans is always possible and often happens. Nonetheless, it must also be possible to be right and successful. If it is not possible ever to be right or successful, then being right or successful have no meaning. If it is impossible under any circumstances to solve an arithmetic problem correctly, then it is impossible to do it incorrectly too. Correctness and incorrectness have no meaning, if it is possible to be both correct and incorrect at the same time.

Being consistent, then, is very important to us. Without consistency we cannot know anything or make intelligent choices about how to act. An important part of the art of reasoning is to know when we and others hold consistent beliefs and when we do not.

Exercise 3   Student_____

Because there is an inconsistent belief for every belief we hold, there must be a way of expressing beliefs and their contradictions. In English we often use "not," "no," "none," and other negative words and phrases to express the contradictions to our beliefs. For example, I might hold a belief about the medieval ruler Charlemagne expressed in the sentence

[a] Charlemagne was a great supporter of education.

The contradictory of this belief could be expressed by the sentence

[b] Charlemagne was not a great supporter of education.

We say that [b] expresses the negation of what [a] expresses. Truth value is the truth or falsity of a belief. The negation of a belief always has an opposite truth value to the affirmation of the belief. In other words, if [a] is true, then [b] must be false. If, on the other hand, [a] is false, then [b] must be true.

For each of the beliefs expressed by the following sentences, write out a sentence expressing a contradictory belief. Be sure that your sentence expressing the contradictory belief expresses a belief which **must** have an opposite truth value to the one given.

1.   Charlemagne was proclaimed Emperor of the West by the pope.

_____

2.   Charlemagne was unable to read or write.

_____

3.   Some of Charlemagne's policies were just.

_____

4.   Charlemagne defeated the Saxons.

_____

5.   Charlemagne admired well-educated monks.

_____

- 9 -

§3 Saying What is True or False

If argument is a process of giving reasons in support of the truth of a conclusion, then the parts from which an argument is constructed must be capable of expressing what is true or false about the real world. We have already seen that arguments are composed of premises and conclusions and that these express beliefs. We must now take a closer look at these components of argument and ask just what they are.

It is clear that they must be some use of language and that they must concern what is true or false. What is true or false is expressed in language by means of sentences such as "Oxygen burns" or "George is guilty." Such sentences may be used on one occasion to express conclusions and on another to express premises. They may even be used as parts of larger sentences, for example, "If oxygen burns, then the phlogiston theory is wrong" or "Either George is guilty or she is." In logic, we are not so much interested in the sentences themselves (as grammatical units), but in what the sentences express and it is this that is true or false. The term "proposition" is used to indicate what such sentences express.

The distinction between sentence and proposition can be understood by considering the fact that the same sentence, spoken or written on different occasions or on the same occasion but by different persons, might express quite different propositions. For example, the sentence "My back hurts" might express a true proposition when uttered by me now, but false tomorrow. Further, this sentence might express true, but quite different propositions, when spoken by two different people. On the other hand, the two quite different sentences "Mary hit the mailman" and "The mailman was hit by Mary" express the same proposition. The same point might be made by comparing sentences in different languages. For example, "Brutus Caesarum occidit" and "Brutus killed Caesar" are clearly different sentences with different grammatical structures, the first in Latin and the second in English. Both, however, express the same proposition.

Even though propositions are expressed by sentences, not all sentences express propositions. This is because we use language for many different purposes. We use it to make requests and give commands, to express our wishes, to ask questions, and so on. Nonetheless, one of the most important things we do with language is to say what is true or false of the real world. Thus, sentences which say what is true or false express propositions.

Consider the following English sentences and determine whether each expresses a proposition or some other use of language.

1.   Brother William is a Franciscan friar.

      proposition ___   not a proposition ___

2.   Does Brother William know how to use an astrolabe?

      proposition ___   not a proposition ___

3.   Tell Brother William to bring me his astrolabe.

      proposition ___   not a proposition ___

4.   Brother William has constructed an astrolabe.

      proposition ___   not a proposition ___

5.   Brother William used an Arabic astrolabe as a model in constructing his own.

      proposition ___   not a proposition ___

6.   Will the Prior show Brother William's astrolabe to our visitors?

      proposition ___   not a proposition ___

7.   Brother William is the only friar in our community who is able to use the astrolabe.

      proposition __   not a proposition __

8.   I wish Brother William would show me how to use the astrolabe.

      proposition __   not a proposition __

9.   Brother William says that the Sultan sent an astrolabe to the Emperor at Constantinople as a gift.

      proposition __   not a proposition __

10.   Either Brother William constructed this astrolabe or Brother Hugh did.

      proposition __   not a proposition __

11.   Instruct Brother William to demonstrate the use of his astrolabe for the bishop.

      proposition __   not a proposition __

12.   I wish I could read Arabic astronomical treatises as Brother William can.

      proposition __   not a proposition __

13.   Brother William promised me that he would teach me to use the astrolabe.

      proposition __   not a proposition __

14.   Promise me, Brother William, that you will teach me to use the astrolabe.

      proposition __   not a proposition __

15.   Would that I could use the astrolabe!

      proposition __   not a proposition __

16. If Brother William sends his astrolabe to Sir Robert, then we will not be able to demonstrate it for the bishop.

    proposition ___ not a proposition ___

17. Both Brother William and Brother Hugh have written treatises on the astrolabe.

    proposition ___ not a proposition ___

18. Return the astrolabe to Brother William's room.

    proposition ___ not a proposition ___

19. Have you returned the astrolabe to Brother William's room?

    proposition ___ not a proposition ___

20. When Brother William demonstrates his astrolabe to the king, he will become famous.

    proposition ___ not a proposition ___

Every proposition is a use of language capable of expressing what is true or false. Another way of saying this is that every proposition has truth value. Truth value is the truth or falsity of a proposition. There are only two possible truth values: **true** and **false**. Thus, every proposition is either true or false. This, of course, does not mean that we always know what the truth value of a given proposition is. We may or may not, but we do know that it must be either one or the other.

Some propositions are simple. They have no smaller parts which have truth value. The following sentence, for example, expresses a simple proposition:

[a] Alcuin was a learned man.

No smaller part of it is capable of having truth value. ("Alcuin" is neither true nor false, it is simply a name of someone. "Was a learned man" by itself lacks truth value, because it cannot say what is true or false until it is linked with a subject.) Some propositions, on the other hand, are complex. They have smaller parts which do have truth value. Consider this sentence:

[b] Both Alcuin and John were learned men.

It actually expresses two propositions connected by a "both . . . and" to form a longer more complex proposition. The two smaller propositions are "Alcuin was a learned man" and "John was a learned man."

For each of the following sentences, determine whether it expresses a simple or complex proposition.

1.   Alcuin and John were Irish.

            simple ___   complex ___

2.   Alcuin was a learned monk.

            simple ___   complex ___

3.   If Alcuin is invited to Charlemagne's court, he will establish a school there.

            simple ___   complex ___

4.   John the Scot wrote many learned treatises in Latin.

       simple ___ complex ___

5.   Ratramnus seriously disagrees with Macarius on the nature of propositions.

       simple ___ complex ___

6.   Either Ratramnus is right or Macarius is right.

       simple ___ complex ___

7.   Macarius is not right about the nature of propositions.

       simple ___ complex ___

8.   It cannot be that both Ratramnus and Macarius are right about the nature of propositions.

       simple ___ complex ___

9.   Alcuin will direct the new school or John will return to Ireland.

       simple ___ complex ___

10.   John the Scot translated many Greek books into Latin.

       simple ___ complex ___

Exercise 6   Student_____

The following sentences express complex propositions. For each one, write out the smaller propositions which compose it.

1.   If John returns to Ireland, the emperor will have to close the school.

   _____

   _____

2.   The emperor will choose either Alcuin or John to establish the court school.

   _____

   _____

3.   Both Ratramnus of Corbie and John the Scot read Greek.

   _____

   _____

4.   Whenever Alcuin speaks, the emperor listens humbly.

   _____

   _____

§4 How Can a Proposition be True or False?

What makes it possible for a proposition to say what is true or false of the real world? The answer to this question has to do with the way in which a proposition is constructed. All propositions have two different kinds of parts. One sort of part tells us what the proposition is about--it carries the content or subject-matter of the proposition. The other kind of part tells us how we are to understand what the proposition is saying about this subject-matter.

The parts of a proposition which tell us what a proposition is about are called "terms." Consider the following proposition:

[1] All students of Alcuin can read Latin.

This proposition is about certain people, namely those who are students of a man named Alcuin. It is also about a certain ability that they share, namely the ability to read Latin. The first of these can be called the subject term, because it picks out a subject about which we can say something. What we say of the subject is that which the second term contains. This second term can be called the predicate term, because it predicates or attributes something of the subject. So, it is possible for propositions to be about something because they have two terms: one which picks out a subject and another which predicates something of that subject.

It is important that we be able to pick out the terms of a proposition. If we cannot do this, then we will be unable to understand what is being said of the real world. If we cannot understand what is being said of the real world, then we cannot know whether the proposition saying it is true or false. In [1], then, the terms can be clearly expressed by the following:

[t1] people who are students of Alcuin

and

[t2] people who can read Latin.

There is more to a proposition than its terms. Propositions also have logical parts. These are expressed by words and phrases which tell us how the terms of the proposition go together or do not go together. In [1] the word "all" tells us that being a person who is a student of Alcuin goes together with being a person who can read Latin. It also tells us that these terms go together in every case, not in just some cases. All propositions not only have two terms--which tell us what the proposition is about--but also have quality and quantity. The quality of the proposition tells us whether the terms go together (affirmative quality) or do not go together (negative quality). The quantity of a proposition tells us how often or in how many cases the terms go together (or do not go together). In [1], both the quality and quantity of the proposition are expressed by the logical word "all."

It is the fact that a proposition must have two terms as well as quality and quantity that makes it possible for it to say what is true or false of the real world. If what the proposition says in presenting to us its terms understood with respect to a particular quantity and quality corresponds to the way the world really exists, then what the proposition says is true; otherwise, false. Thus, looking at [1] again, if being a person who is a student of Alcuin really goes together with being a person who is able to read Latin in every case, then [1] is true. If these terms really do not go together in every case, then [1] is false.

An example of a proposition with a negative quality is:

[2] None of Alcuin's students can read Greek.

Like every proposition, [2] has two terms: "people who are students of Alcuin" and "people who can read Greek." The word "none" expresses both the negative quality as well as the universal (that is, referring to every case) quantity of [2]. Thus, if being a person who is a student of Alcuin does not really go with being a person who can read Greek in every case, then [2] is true; otherwise false.

For each of the following propositions, write out the two terms composing it.

1.   No student of Alcuin is a student of Sedulius.

      first term: _____

      second term: _____

2.   All of Alcuin's students are very intelligent.

      first term: _____

      second term: _____

3.   Alcuin was the most brilliant teacher of his time.

      first term: _____

      second term: _____

4.   Some monks are students of Alcuin.

      first term: _____

      second term: _____

5.   No one who can read Hebrew was a student of Alcuin.

      first term: _____

      second term: _____

§5 Quality and Quantity

We have already discussed the difference between simple and complex propositions. All simple propositions are categorical--that is, they say what is true or false without attaching any conditions or qualifications. Propositions which say what is true or false on the basis of a condition or qualification are called "conditional." Conditional propositions will be discussed later. Because all propositions are composed of two terms, a categorical proposition says that the two terms either go together or do not go together (affirmative quality or negative quality) and do so either in every case (universal quantity) or in some cases (existential quantity). Thus, there are four basic forms of categorical proposition:

Universal Affirmative Propositions

A categorical proposition affirming that both terms apply together in all cases is universal and affirmative. If the schematic letters F and G stand for any two terms, then universal affirmatives have the following form:

All F is G.

So do these examples:

[1] Everything the master said is true.

and

[2] All whales are mammals.

Universal affirmative propositions are often expressed by sentences beginning with a word or phrase expressing the universal quantifier such as "all," "every," "everybody," "everything," "every man," "every woman," "every person," "any," "anybody," "anything," "each," "only," or "none but." The presence of one of these words, however, is not necessary for a sentence to express a universal affirmative. The proposition "Birds fly," for example, is both universal and affirmative, because it affirms an attribute (the ability to fly) to all birds.

Universal Negative Propositions

A categorical proposition which denies that two terms apply together in all cases is called a universal negative. If the schematic letters F and G stand for any two terms, then universal negatives have this form:

No F is G.

So do the following examples:

[4] Nothing the master said was very interesting.

[5] No whales are fish.

Universal negative propositions are often expressed by sentences beginning with some negative form of the universal quantifier such as "no," "none," "there is no," "there are no," "not any," or "nothing." Other ways of expressing a universal negative, however, are also possible. Consider this example:

[6] Birds lack dorsal fins.

It, too, is a universal negative, because it refers to all birds and denies an attribute of them all; that is, it is the same as saying "No bird has a dorsal fin."

Existential Affirmative Propositions

A categorical proposition which affirms that two terms apply in some cases is called an existential affirmative. Using the schematic letters F and G to stand for any two terms, an existential affirmative has the form:

Some F is G.

So do these examples:

[7] Something the master said was true.

[8] Some whales are mammals.

Existential affirmative propositions are often expressed by sentences beginning with some form of the existential quantifier such as "some," "somebody," "something," "there is," "there are," "a," "an," or "at least one." As can be seen by the last three forms of the existential quantifier, an existential affirmative can be true even if only one subject has the predicate true of it. Consider the following:

[9] Some students respect Master Giles.

It is true if at least one student respects Master Giles. Thus, the existential quantifier refers to at least one subject, and it might also refer to more than one. This logical meaning of the word "some" differs from its grammatical meaning which usually refers to more than one.

Existential Negative Propositions

A categorical proposition which denies that two terms apply in some cases is called an existential negative. If F and G stand for any predicate terms, then existential negatives have the form:

Some F lack G.

So do the examples:

[10] Something Master Giles said was not true.

[11] Some whales are not killer whales.

Existential negatives have a negated second term and assert the existence of something, whose identity is given by the first term, which lacks the property indicated by the second term.

[12] There are problems which even the master cannot solve.

This proposition says that there exist some problems which lack the property of being within the capacity of the master to solve.

For each of the following propositions, indicate which type of categorical proposition it is. Underline any words or phrases which express the quality or quantity of the proposition.

1.   All of Master Gilbert's books are in the library.

        _____

2.   Some of Master Gilbert's students are from Italy.

        _____

3.   Every student must study with Master Gilbert.

        _____

4.   Masters must respect serious students.

        _____

5.   Some students have not read Master Gilbert's books.

        _____

6.   Any student of Master Gilbert is a friend of mine.

        _____

7.   There are students who have not read Master Gilbert's book.

        _____

8.   Everybody who has studied with Master Gilbert understands Plato.

        _____

9.   No student of Master Gilbert is a student of Master Hugh.

        _____

10.   At least one of Master Gilbert's books is in the library.

        _____

11. None of the books in the library were written by our Master.

_____

12. Every one of the books in the library is in Latin.

_____

13. None but the brave question Master Hugh.

_____

14. Students of Master Hugh are unhappy students.

_____

15. Somebody took Master Hugh's book.

_____

16. There is no one who would dare to question Master Hugh.

_____

17. Master Gilbert is an expert on Plato's cosmology.

_____

18. Anything said by Plato is taken seriously by Master Gilbert.

_____

19. No masters take their meals with the novices.

_____

20. There are passages of Master Hugh's book which do not make sense.

_____

The logical form of a proposition does not depend on its subject matter. Another way of saying this is that many different propositions having differing subject matter may share the very same logical form. Consider the following:

> [a] All students of Master Hugh read Latin.

> [b] Every Parthian nobleman is an expert horseman.

They are different propositions because they are about different things: [a] is about the students of Master Hugh and their ability to read Latin and [b] is about Parthian noblemen and their expertness in horsemanship. Nonetheless, the two propositions have exactly the same logical form, because they are both universal affirmatives.

The subject matter of a proposition can sometimes distract us from seeing its logical form, especially when it is very complex. In these cases it is useful to display the logical form of a proposition by making a schematic representation of it. This can be done by replacing the real terms of the proposition with schematic letters--one distinct letter for each distinct term. This makes it easy to see what the form of a proposition is. Thus, if we replace the first term in both [a] and [b] with the letter F and the second term in each with the letter G and use "all" to represent the universal quantifier, then we can show that both propositions have the form:

> All F is G.

This, of course, is the form of any universal affirmative proposition.

Let us agree to represent the universal quantifier in affirmative propositions by "all" and in universal negative propositions by "no." Let us also agree to represent the existential quantifier by "some" and the negation of a term by "not." Using these conventions, we can uniformly schematize any categorical proposition. The four basic forms of categorical proposition, then, can be schematized like this:

[A]	Universal affirmative:	All F is G
[B]	Universal negative:	No F is G
[C]	Existential affirmative:	Some F is G
[D]	Existential negative:	Some F is not G

Using these conventions, give a schematic representation of the following propositions. Use the schematic letters F and G to stand in for the terms.

1. Normans speak a kind of French.

    _____

2. There are Greeks who can speak Arabic.

    _____

3. Some Arabic-speaking people are Christian.

    _____

4. Any master at the university can speak Latin.

    _____

5. Only Germans speak German.

    _____

6. Everybody who travels to Rome is eager to leave.

    _____

7. The Roman emperors at Constantinople always live in the Great Palace.

    _____

8. There are Normans who do not respect Saxons.

    _____

9. Some Norman scholars have studied with the Arabic philosophers at Salerno.

    _____

10. Normans are warlike.

    _____

§6 Diagraming Propositions

The Swiss mathematician Leonhard Euler (1707-1783) first devised a system of diagrams to represent the forms of quantified categorical propositions. A similar system was later invented by the British mathematician John Venn (1834-1923) and this is the system most commonly used.

The terms in a proposition are represented by circles which may be thought of as representing the class or group of those things having the property in question. The following diagram represents the class or group of things having the property F true of them:

Because the four basic types of categorical propositions have two terms, a diagram of any one of them will be composed of two circles, one for each term. Further, the circles will have to overlap in such a way that the diagram will be divided into areas or regions each of which represents a logical possibility of how a given combination of the terms can be true of some subject. For two terms, there are four possible combinations: F is true of the subject and G is not, G is true and F is not, both F and G are true, and neither F nor G are true of the subject. This can be seen by plotting the possibilities on a two-termed diagram:

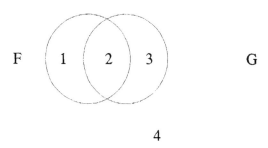

1 - F is true, but not G
2 - both F and G are true
3 - G is true, but not F
4 - neither F nor G are true

These represent all the possibilities for two terms and drawing our diagram in this way shows this.

On a diagram which allows for all the logical possibilities for two terms we can represent each of the four basic categorical propositions. The universal affirmative "All whales are mammals" says that everything that is a whale is also a mammal. Thus, it rules out there being whales which are not mammals. This can be represented by a Venn diagram like this:

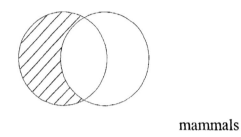

whales   mammals

The region which represents whales which are not mammals is shaded to show that there is nothing there. Shading a region of a Venn diagram rules out the logical possibility represented by that region. All universal affirmative propositions would be diagramed in a similar way.

The universal negative "No whales are fish" says that there is nothing which is both a whale and a fish. Thus, it rules out there being whales of which it is also true to say that they are fish. That is:

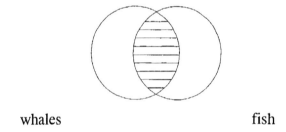

whales   fish

The region which is both whales and fish is shaded out to show that there is nothing there--the logical possibility of a thing being both a whale and a fish is ruled out.

The existential affirmative "Some whales are mammals" says that there is at least one thing which is both a whale and a mammal. This can be represented by a Venn diagram using a "+" to mark the region which represents the logical possibility which is true for at least one object:

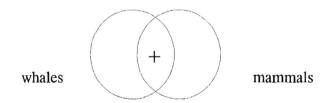

whales   mammals

The existential negative "Some whales are not gray whales" says that there is at least one thing which is a whale but not a gray whale. This can be represented by a diagram placing the "+" in the region that represents the logical possibility of being a whale without being a gray whale. Thus:

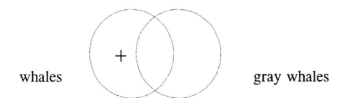

Notice that Venn diagrams say no more and no less than the propositions they represent. To summarize:

All F is G.

No F is G.

Some F is G.

Some F is not G.

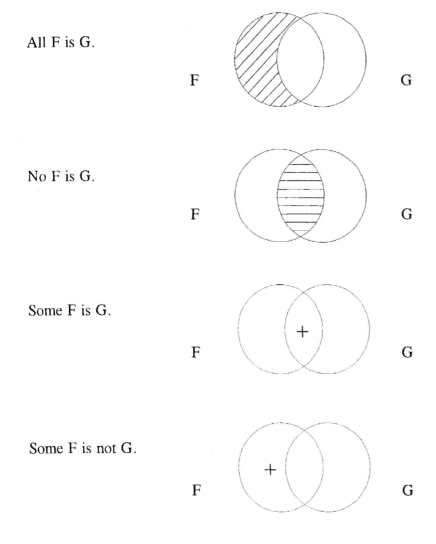

As an example of analyzing the logical form of categorical propositions, let us use a saying of the ancient Chinese philosopher Lao-Tzu:

A sensible man does not argue.

Our first task is to determine what sort of proposition this is. It is categorical because it states something without conditions. If it is categorical, then it has to be one of the four basic types of categorical propositions. Because each type has both quantity (universal or existential) and quality (affirmative or negative), we must determine its quantity and quality before we can diagram it. Does the proposition apply only to some people or all people? Clearly, Lao-Tzu is _not_ saying that some sensible men do not argue, because he is giving us an aphorism. Thus, the proposition is not existential and so must be universal. Is he universally affirming or denying something? The presence of a "not" is a clue: he is saying that something is not true of all sensible men. Thus, this proposition is a negation. The next step is to determine what the terms are. Clearly, the proposition is about <u>sensible men</u> and says something about them. What it says about them is that they do not <u>argue</u>. So, the first term must be <u>being a sensible man</u>. The word "not" is a sign of negation and so is a logical word and not a term. This leaves <u>man who argues</u> as the second term. Having determined both the quantity and quality as well as the terms in this way, we can go on to rephrase the proposition to make its logical form more obvious:

No sensible man is a man who argues.

When we do this, we can see that the proposition is a universal negation which fits the pattern: No F is G. This gives us what we need to draw our diagram:

being a sensible man   being a man who argues

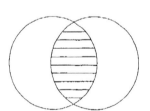

We can apply this method to some other famous sayings:

1. Nothing is more useful than silence. (Menander)

    rephrased: No thing is a thing more useful than silence.

    things   items more useful than silence

    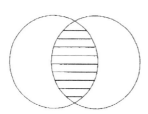

2. The absent are always in the wrong. (Philippe Destouches)

    rephrased: All absent people are people who are in the wrong.

    people who are absent   people who are in the wrong

    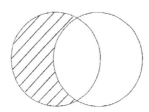

3. Who does not know the value of words will never come to understand his fellow men. (Confucius)

    rephrased: All people who do not know the value of words are people who will never come to understand their fellows.

    people who do not know   people who will never come
    know the value of words   to understand their fellows

For each of the following propositions, draw a Venn diagram to represent its logical form.

1.   All Norman knights are brave.

2.   Some Normans are living in southern Italy.

3.   Some Normans living in southern Italy want to return to Normandy.

4.   There are Normans who are not knights.

5.   No Norman dishonors his parents.

6.   Normans are treacherous.

7.   There are Normans who are treacherous.

8.   At least one Roman historian wrote of the Parthian Wars.

9.   None of the Romans living in Parthia wants to return to Rome.

10.   Every Roman living in Parthia wants to return to Rome.

11.   Only some of the people living in Constantinople are Roman citizens.

12.   Each Roman living in Alexandria must pay respects to the governor.

13.   Some of the Romans living in Alexandria do not want to return to Rome.

14.   All Romans living in Alexandria have visited the governor's house.

15.   There are Romans living in Alexandria who lack honesty.

16.   Not all of the Romans living in Alexandria are soldiers.

17.   All of the Romans living in Alexandria are not returning to Rome.

18.   Every Roman governor of Alexandria has been appointed by the Senate.

19.   Only governors appointed by the Senate are legal.

20.   None of the Romans living in Alexandria approve the new law.

21.   Art never expresses anything but itself. (Oscar Wilde)

22.   No one is exempt from talking nonsense. (Montaigne)

23.   He who complains, sins. (St. Francis de Sales)

24. All knowledge is of the universal. (Aristotle)

25. Nobody has money who ought to have it. (Benjamin Disraeli)

26. Those who know do not tell; those who tell do not know. (Lao-Tzu)

27. There are men who are happy without knowing it. (Vauvenargues)

28. No man was ever wise by chance. (Seneca)

29. Blessed are the peacemakers. (Jesus)

§7 Propositional Relationships

The four basic types of categorical propositions stand in certain relationships to each other such that, given any one of them, you know something about another of them. For example, if you know that "All F is G" is true, then you also know that "Some F are not G" is not true. There are four such relationships between categorical propositions and they can be illustrated on a kind of diagram usually called The Square of Opposition. Since the ancient Greek philosopher Aristotle (384-322BC) was the first to scientifically discuss these propositional relationships, this diagram is sometimes called Aristotle's Square. These relationships are illustrated below and each type of relation is discussed in detail in the pages which follow.

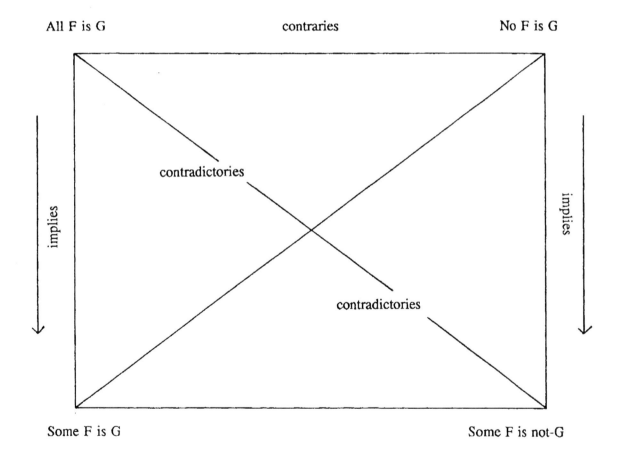

ARISTOTLE'S SQUARE

Contrariety

Sometimes we know from the form of a certain categorical proposition that a certain other proposition cannot be true at the same time as our first proposition is true. This is the case when the one proposition is the contrary of the other.

Strictly speaking, two propositions are contraries if, and only if, they can never both be true, but can both be false. A look at Aristotle's Square shows that a universal affirmative and a universal negative are contraries. This is because, if "All F is G" is true, then "No F is G" must be false and if "No F is G" is true, then "All F is G" must be false. But they both might be false. Consider the following propositions:

[1] All philosophers have beards.

[2] No philosophers have beards.

These are contrary propositions, because both of these propositions cannot be true together. But both can be false if, for example, some philosophers have beards and some do not.

Implication

One proposition implies another if whenever one is true the other is also true. The proposition which implies the other is said to be superimplicant to the other. The proposition which is implied by the other is said to be subimplicant to the one implying it. Thus, "All F is G" implies "Some F is G" and "No F is G" implies "Some F is not G." For example, "All philosophers love to talk" implies "Some philosophers love to talk." Also, "No philosopher can tie his shoes" implies that "Some philosopher cannot tie his shoes." In other words, if the first proposition in each of these pairs is true, the second in each pair must be true. Note, however, that the implication does not work the other way around: the second in each pair does not imply the first in each pair. For example, given that "Some philosophers love to talk" is true, it does not follow that "All philosophers love to talk" must be true.

Contradiction

Two propositions contradict each other if, and only if, they can never have the same truth value. Thus, "All F is G" contradicts "Some F is not G" and "No F is G" is the contradictory of "Some F is G." The following propositions, for example, contradict each other:

[9] All philosophers love to think.

[10] Some philosophers hate to think.

They can never both be true at the same time, nor can they both be false at the same time. If the first is true, then the second must be false and, if the second is true, then the first must be false. Contradiction is an important logical concept. To try to say that two propositions which are contradictory are true together is to say something absurd. "Every student failed the exam and some students passed the exam" is not only something which cannot be true, but is nonsense.

Logical Equivalence

Some important relationships between propositions are not represented on Aristotle's square. One of the most important of these is logical equivalence. Two propositions are logically equivalent if, and only if, they always have the same truth value. For example, the following two propositions are logically equivalent:

[11] No Norman king has ever traveled to China.

[12] All Norman kings have never traveled to China.

If [11] is true, then [12] must be true. If [11] is false, then [12] must be false. In the same way the truth value of [12] will determine the truth value of [11].

Conversion

The converse of a proposition is a proposition of the same form with the order of the terms reversed. Thus, "All F is G" is the converse of "All G is F." Universal negatives and existential affirmatives are equivalent to their converses. But universal affirmatives and existential negatives are not. For example, the two propositions "No Roman is a Greek" and its converse "No Greek is a Roman" are equivalent. Equivalent propositions always have the same truth value. Thus, if it is true that "No Roman is a Greek" it must also be true that "No Greek is a Roman." Given that we know a certain proposition is true, we can conclude to the truth of a proposition which is equivalent to it. As noted above, not all converse pairs of propositions are equivalent. The proposition "All Romans are brave" is not equivalent to its converse "All brave people are Romans" since there might be brave people who are not Roman even if all the Romans in existence are brave. In other words, the truth of the first proposition does not allow us immediately to infer the truth of the second proposition which is its converse.

Immediate Inference

We have already discussed the kind of relationship which can exist between propositions called implication. In fact, this relationship is one of inference or drawing a conclusion. If we know that a certain proposition is true, then we can conclude that its subimplicant is true. For example, if we know that "All of Master Giles' students know Latin" is true, then we can immediately conclude that "Some of Master Giles' students know Latin" must be true. So, implication is a kind of argument with premise and conclusion. Since we have here only one premise from which we can immediately conclude something, we have a special kind of argument known as immediate inference.

Logical Validity

Proper implications are valid arguments. A valid argument is one in which the relationship between the premise or premises and the conclusion is one of necessity. In other words, in a valid argument, when all of the premises are true, then the conclusion _must_ be true. It is impossible in a valid argument that the conclusion be false when all of the premises are true. Arguments which are valid in this way are called formal arguments and are the strongest possible kinds of arguments, because they establish their conclusions in the strongest or best possible way. Formally valid arguments prove their conclusions in such a way that if there is no doubt about the truth of the premises, then there can be no doubt about the truth of the conclusion. Arguments which leave open the possibility that the conclusion is false even when all the premises are true are, therefore, not formally valid.

We know from Aristotle's Square that universal affirmatives imply existential affirmatives and that universal negatives imply existential negatives. If we know that a universal proposition is true, then we can infer (argue to) the corresponding (that is, having the same quality and terms) existential proposition. Let us agree to write arguments in such a way that the premise or premises are written above a line and the conclusion below the line. Think of this line as representing the word "therefore." The following two arguments are valid:

All penguins live in the Antarctic.
Some penguins live in the Antarctic.

No penguins live in the Arctic.
Some penguins do not live in the Arctic.

Notice that implication does not hold from existential to universal. For example, the following is an invalid argument:

Some penguins lay their eggs on New Georgia Island.
All penguins lay their eggs on New Georgia Island.

The reason why this is an invalid argument is that the premise might be true while the conclusion is false. In other words, the truth of the premise does not guarantee (make necessary) the truth of the conclusion.

Logical equivalence provides us with another kind of immediate inference. We can immediately infer (argue) from a proposition to its logical equivalent, because if a proposition is true, then its equivalent must be true. Thus, the following are valid arguments:

No penguins live in the Arctic.
Nothing that lives in the Arctic is a penguin.

Some penguins live in the Antarctic.
Some things living in the Antarctic are penguins.

No penguins live in the Arctic.
All penguins do not live in the Arctic.

You can prove that these are valid arguments by drawing a Venn diagram for each premise and each conclusion. You will find that the diagram for each premise is identical with that for each conclusion. Identity of Venn diagrams shows logical equivalence.

Exercise 11   Student_____

For each pair of propositions, use Venn diagrams to determine whether the pair is logically equivalent. (Draw a Venn diagram for <u>each</u> proposition and circle the correct answer.)

1.   None of Master Giles' students have read Plato's book.

        None of those who have read Plato's book are Master Giles' students.

                                                        equivalent/not equivalent

2.   Every one of Master Giles' students has studied geometry.

        Everyone who has studied geometry is a student of Master Giles.

                                                        equivalent/not equivalent

3.   Some of the emperor's knights are not brave.

        Some of those who are not brave are the emperor's knights.

                                                        equivalent/not equivalent

4.   No planets have circular orbits.

        Nothing with circular orbits are planets.

                                                    equivalent/not equivalent

5.   Some heavenly bodies do not orbit the sun.

        No heavenly bodies orbit the sun.

                                                    equivalent/not equivalent

6.   No planets have circular orbits.

        All planets lack circular orbits.

                                                    equivalent/not equivalent

Exercise 12   Student_____

If "All roads lead to Rome" is true, what can we deduce about the truth values of the following propositions?

1.   Some roads lead to Rome.

      true/false Why? _____

2.   No roads lead to Rome.

      true/false Why? _____

3.   Some roads don't lead to Rome.

      true/false Why? _____

If "No roads lead to Utopia" is true, what can we deduce about the truth values of the following propositions?

4.   Nothing that leads to Utopia is a road.

      true/false Why? _____

5.   All roads lead to Utopia.

      true/false Why? _____

6.   Some road does not lead to Utopia.

      true/false Why? _____

7.   Some road leads to Utopia.

      true/false Why? _____

8.   There exist roads that lead to Utopia.

      true/false Why? _____

§8 Categorical Arguments

Mediate Inference

In the previous section, we discussed immediate inference, which is the kind of argument where we can conclude that a proposition is true on the basis of the truth of one other proposition. This kind of argument is called immediate because our inference is based on knowing the logical form of one proposition alone. This proposition is, then, the premise of an argument which leads us immediately to the necessity of a certain conclusion.

A more common type of argument is that in which the truth of the conclusion is inferred from more than one premise. In this kind of argument the inference to the conclusion is not immediate from one premise alone, but is mediated by another premise or even several premises. There are many kinds of mediate inference, but the most common involving categorical propositions is the categorical syllogism. This is the type of argument that Aristotle thought was the most important for scientific reasoning and his treatment of it formed the core of the study of logic for many centuries, up to our own time. We will study other types of mediate inference later in this course. For now, we will focus our attention on the categorical syllogism alone.

The Categorical Syllogism

A categorical syllogism (often simply called "syllogism") is an argument containing three categorical propositions and three distinct terms. One of the propositions is the conclusion--which is, of course, the proposition which the argument is meant to prove. The other two propositions are premises--which are, of course, the reasons given in support of the conclusion. Within these three propositions the three terms are distributed (arranged) in a particular way. It is important to note that all syllogisms have some distribution of no more than, and no fewer than, three terms. This means that a given term may appear more than once in a syllogism. The following argument patterns are typical of syllogistic form:

[1] All F is G.
    All G is H.
    All F is H.

[2] Some H is F.
    No G is F.
    Some G is not H.

[3] All F is G.
    Some F is not H.
    Some G is not H.

The first thing to notice about these examples is that they are, of course, not real syllogisms, but only schematic representations of syllogisms. Like all types of arguments, real syllogisms would be stated in ordinary language and would be about something. These representations of syllogisms are not about anything, because the content-bearing ordinary-language terms have been replaced by schematic letters. An example of a real syllogism is:

[4]   All Norman knights are brave horsemen.
             <u>All brave horsemen are dependable in battle.</u>
             All Norman knights are dependable in battle.

Of course, there are many possible syllogisms which have the same logical form as this one (perhaps an infinite number), so if we want to study the logical form of this syllogism and others like it we can study a schematic representation of it. Our example [1] above is a representation of this syllogism.

The next thing to notice about our schematic representations of syllogisms is the conventions we will use to represent the logical form of these arguments. We place the conclusion, the proposition which the syllogism is supposed to prove, below a line and the other two propositions, our premises, above the line. Thus, the line shows which proposition is the conclusion and which are the premises and can be thought of as representing the word "therefore."

Create a schematic representation for each of the categorical syllogisms below. Use the schematic letters F, G, and H to represent the terms.

1.   All roads lead to Rome. Everything that leads to Rome was built by the Romans. Therefore, all roads were built by the Romans.

2.   Some Norman knights are veterans of the Sicilian Wars. Some veterans of the Sicilian Wars are now living in Naples. Therefore, some Norman knights are now living in Naples.

3.   No Roman would live in Bactria willingly. Some people living in Bactria are Roman. So, some people living in Bactria are there against their will.

4.   Every Roman who has done garrison duty in Mauretania learns to hate the place. Anyone who hates Mauretania also hates Tingis. Therefore, every Roman who has served in the Mauretanian garrison dislikes Tingis.

5.   All Romans are wine drinkers and some beer drinkers are not wine drinkers. Thus, some beer drinkers are not Roman.

6.   No Norman drinks mead and all Saxons drink mead and that is why no Norman is a Saxon.

§9 Testing Syllogisms for Validity

While all categorical syllogisms are arguments, not all forms of syllogism are valid arguments. In §7 we discussed the concept of validity as it applies to arguments and it was there noted that in a valid argument, where all the premises are true, the conclusion must be true. It is this kind of necessity that a valid syllogism possesses: the truth of the premises guarantees the truth of the conclusion. As in all arguments, the validity of a syllogism depends, not on what it is about--its subject matter--but on its logical form (see §5). Thus, in order to determine the validity of syllogisms, a technique is needed to test whether the logical form of any particular syllogism is a valid or invalid form. Venn diagrams can provide such a technique.

We have already used Venn diagrams to represent the logical form of propositions. These diagrams can also be used to represent the logical form of syllogisms, because such arguments are composed of propositions. Just as in a categorical proposition there are two terms and so a diagram of it must have two circles, in a similar way a diagram representing a syllogism must have three circles because syllogisms always have three terms. Again, just as in a diagram for a two-termed proposition the circles must overlap to represent all the logically possible combination of two terms, so in a syllogistic diagram the three circles must overlap in such a way so as to represent all the logically possible combinations of three terms. Thus,

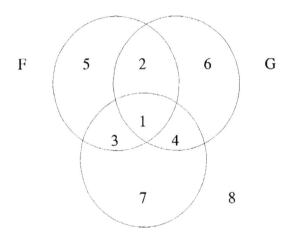

1 - F, G, H
2 - F, G, not-H
3 - F, not-G, H
4 - not-F, G, H
5 - F, not-G, not-H
6 - not-F, G, not-H
7 - not-F, not-G, H
8 - not-F, not-G, not-H

On a diagram of this sort, we can plot the premises of a syllogism in the same way that we diagramed propositions. Let us consider, for example, a syllogism of form [1]:

[1]   All F is G.
        All G is H.
        All F is H.

It will be diagramed like this:

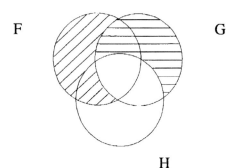

Having diagramed the two premises, we can test the syllogism for validity by looking to see if our diagram of the premises is, in fact, also a diagram of the conclusion as well. We see that the above diagram not only shows that all F is G and all G is H, but it also shows that all F is II, because the only part of F which has not been ruled out (shaded out) is within H. But we created this diagram by plotting our premises alone, not by plotting our conclusion separately. It is in making a diagram of our premises that we have also made a diagram of our conclusion. In effect, we have assumed that both of our premises are true (we diagramed them) and, having made this assumption, we find that we have also shown that our conclusion must true as well (we end up with a diagram of that too). This is, of course, just what a valid argument is: if all the premises are true, then the conclusion must be true. Another example, this time with universal negatives in it is:

[2]   All F is G.
        No G is H.
        No H is F.

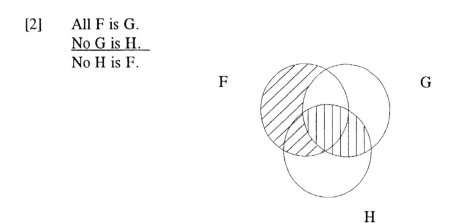

Again we see that this syllogism is valid, because in plotting both of the premises, we have in fact also plotted the conclusion.

Syllogistic diagrams involving existential propositions work in a similar way as can be seen from the following examples.

[3]   All F is G.
        Some F is H.
        Some G is H

Again, we see that this syllogism is valid, because the " + " shows that there is something that is both G and H and this is just what the conclusion says. Not all diagraming involving existential propositions is so straightforward. Consider the following:

[4]   Some H is F.
        No G is F.
        Some G is not-H.

Plotting the first premise is a problem, because, by itself, it does not tell us whether the some H which is F is also G. If it is also G, we would place our cross in region 1 in the center of the diagram; if, on the other hand, it isn't also G, our cross will go in region 3, to the left of center. So, where do we put the cross? The best we can do is to show on our diagram that the first premise says that there is something in either region 1 or region 3, but we don't yet know which. This can be shown by a bar which "straddles the fence" separating the two regions:

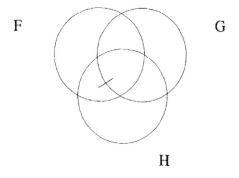

In the case of syllogism [4], the second premise determines the issue for us because it says that there is nothing in region 1. Thus, we can change our bar to a cross in region 3. (If the first premise is true and there is something which is both H and F and the second premise is also true that there is nothing which is both G and F, then the only possibility is that the something which is both H and F must be so without also being G.) So the complete diagram looks like this:

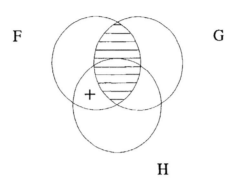

In fact, our complete diagram shows that syllogism [4] is invalid. The conclusion says that there is something which is G but not H and the diagram only shows that there is something which is F and H and rules out there being something which is both G and H. In other words, it does not show that there is some G (there is no cross in any G region) outside of H. Consider another example:

[5]   Every male member of the Fibianus family must serve in the Roman Senate.
        Some Fibianus males are not virtuous.
        Therefore, some Roman senators are not virtuous.

This argument has the following logical form:

All F is G.
Some F is not H.
Some G is not H.

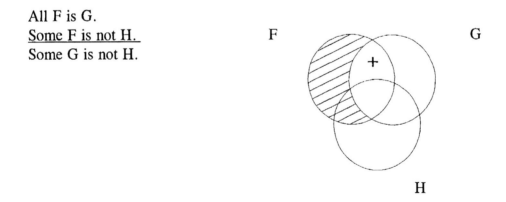

The Venn diagram for this syllogism shows that it is valid, that is, if the premises are all true, the conclusion must be true. This is clear from the fact that the cross appears in G but outside of H, showing that there is something that is G but not H (someone is a Roman senator, but not virtuous).

- 60 -

To summarize the Venn diagram method for testing the validity of syllogisms: (1) construct a diagram consisting of three intersecting circles; (2) label each circle with a term letter; (3) plot the first premise; (4) plot the second premise; (5) check to see whether the diagram is also a plotting of the conclusion (that is, whether the diagram guarantees the truth of the conclusion). If the diagram is in fact a representation of the conclusion, the syllogism is valid. If not, the syllogism is invalid.

Use Venn diagrams to determine which of the following syllogistic forms are valid and which are invalid. (Draw a Venn diagram for each and circle the correct answer.)

1.   All G is H.
      <u>All F is G.</u>
      All F is H.

                                                               valid/invalid

2.   All G is H.
      <u>Some F is G.</u>
      Some F is H.

                                                               valid/invalid

3.   All G is H.
      <u>No F is G.</u>
      No F is H.

                                                               valid/invalid

4.   No G is H.
      <u>All F is G.</u>
      No F is H.

                                                               valid/invalid

5. No G is H.
    No F is G.
    All F is H.

    valid/invalid

6. Some G are not H.
    No F are G.
    Some F are not H.

    valid/invalid

7. Some F is H.
    Some H is G.
    Some F is G.

    valid/invalid

8. All F is H.
    All H is not G.
    All F is G.

    valid/invalid

9. All F is G.
    All G is H.
    All H is F.

                                                        valid/invalid

10. All F is not G.
    All G is not H.
    All F is not H.

                                                        valid/invalid

Schematize the following syllogisms and use Venn diagrams to test for validity. (Create a schematic representation and draw a Venn diagram for each argument. Then circle the correct answer.)

1. No Romans survived the battle of Adrianople and all the heavy cavalry did survive. Therefore, none of the heavy cavalry was Roman.

    valid/invalid

2. Some Roman provincial governors receive their appointments from the Senate and some receive their appointments from the emperor. Thus, some Roman governors are not appointed by the emperor.

    valid/invalid

3. All Roman ambassadors to Parthia have been assassinated and all those who were assassinated were found to carry secret orders from the Roman Governor of Syria. All the Roman ambassadors to Parthia, then, were secretly under orders of the Roman Governor of Syria.

    valid/invalid

Student_____

Read the following dialogue and answer the questions which follow.

On the Sphere

Brother Joseph:	I am sorry to disturb your studies, Master, but I am puzzled by something I read yesterday and I will not rest until the problem is resolved.
Master Albert:	You should not be surprised that a young novice such as yourself, Joseph, is puzzled by what you read. You are only beginning your studies. Have patience and do not allow your many unanswered questions to disturb you. Wisdom will come in due time.
Brother Joseph:	Yes, Reverend Master, I know that patience is a virtue and that I cannot expect to have all of my questions answered at once. Nonetheless, I think that, with your assistance, I may be able to solve this puzzle which so besets me.
Master Albert:	I see that now is the time that your young mind requires guidance. Come then and sit by me. Tell me of your puzzlement.
Brother Joseph:	Yesterday I read in the book of Aristotle that the ancient poets were wrong to deny that the earth is a sphere. Is this wisdom or is it disrespect for the past?
Master Albert:	Tell me, Joseph, do you believe that wisdom is the acknowledging of the truth?
Brother Joseph:	Indeed, I do, Master.
Master Albert:	Do you also agree that the acknowledgment of the truth is worthy of respect?
Brother Joseph:	Yes.
Master Albert:	Thus, you must agree that all wisdom is worthy of respect.
Brother Joseph:	I see that you are correct. Are the ancient poets wrong, then?
Master Albert:	Let us investigate the matter and see. Do you remember the eclipse of the moon which occurred last spring?

Brother Joseph:	Yes, I do. I climbed onto the monastery roof so that I could observe it clearly.
Master Albert:	What was the shape of the shadow which moved across the face of the moon?
Brother Joseph:	It was a curved shadow.
Master Albert:	That is true. Now, what body cast that shadow on the surface of the moon?
Brother Joseph:	Why the earth, of course.
Master Albert:	Good. This will always happen in a lunar eclipse, will it not?
Brother Joseph:	Yes, it will.
Master Albert:	We agree, then, that the earth always casts a curved shadow.
Brother Joseph:	Yes, that will always be true.
Master Albert:	We also know that anything casting a curved shadow must have a curved surface. It follows that the earth must have a curved surface.
Brother Joseph:	I see your point, Master, but this does not prove that the earth is a sphere. It only shows that the earth has at least one curved surface.
Master Albert:	You are quite correct. Nonetheless, I think that we can use the result of our argument to show that the earth is a sphere, if we recall that the earth is a uniform solid body.
Brother Joseph:	I think I see how you intend to argue, Master. We begin by asserting that the earth is a uniform solid body casting a curved shadow.
Master Albert:	Good. Our second premise, then, is the geometrical rule that any uniform solid body casting a curved shadow must be a sphere.
Brother Joseph:	That gives us the conclusion that the earth is a sphere. I see now, Master, that true wisdom does not simply reside in antiquity, but in clear and critical reasoning.

1. At the beginning of the dialogue, Master Albert draws the conclusion that all wisdom is worthy of respect. What are his reasons for thinking that this is true? (Answer this by writing out the two premises of his argument.)

Premise 1: _____

_____

Premise 2: _____

_____

2. What is the logical form of this argument? (Answer this by creating a schematic representation of the argument using the schematic letters W, A, and R to stand in for the terms.)

3. Is this argument valid? (Answer this by drawing a Venn diagram and circling the correct response.)

valid/invalid

4. How does Master Albert prove that the earth must have a curved surface? (Write out the argument in ordinary English sentences.)

Premise 1: _____

_____

Premise 2: _____

_____

Conclusion: _____

_____

5.   What is the form of this argument? (Create a schematic representation of this argument using any schematic letters you wish.)

6.   Is Master Albert's argument that the earth must have a curved surface valid? Prove it.

valid/invalid

7.   What is the argument which finally leads Master Albert and his student Joseph to conclude that the earth must be a sphere? (Write out the argument in ordinary English.)

Premise 1: _____

_____

Premise 2: _____

_____

Conclusion: _____

_____

8.   What is the form of this argument? (Create a schematic representation of the argument using any schematic letters you wish.)

9.   Is it possible to prove that this argument is valid?

      Yes __ No __   If yes, prove it.

§10 Being Elliptical in Argument

In ordinary speech or writing we are often elliptical, that is, we often leave out what is clearly understood without being stated. This is frequently done in argumentation, especially when the form of argument is a categorical syllogism which is a relatively simple type of argument. Thus, we often leave out one of the premises of a syllogism and even sometimes the conclusion when these can easily be supplied by the listener or reader. For example,

All politicians are corrupt, therefore Falangists are corrupt.

It is not difficult to see that this is a shorthand form of the syllogism:

All politicians are corrupt.
All Falangists are politicians.
Therefore, all Falangists are corrupt.

In the shorthand version of the syllogism the second premise was left out, but an educated audience or reader would know that it is to be supplied. Another example is:

No dolphins are fish, since all dolphins are mammals.

This is shorthand for:

No mammals are fish.
All dolphins are mammals.
Thus, no dolphins are fish.

Such shorthand forms of syllogisms are called **enthymemes** or **elliptical syllogisms** and they always supply enough of the syllogism so that what is left out can be easily supplied.

Thus, when we are reading argumentative writing, we must be ready to deal with the problem of ellipsis. This occurs very often in language because when we speak or write we tend to be as economical as we can in our expression. This is done for the sake of convenience and elegance. The analysis of argument to show its logical form and to test it for validity, however, depends on our ability to determine what all of the parts of the argument are. To see how this might be done for an elliptical syllogism, consider the following example taken from the Summa theologica of St. Thomas Aquinas (1225-1274). He is drawing a conclusion about the nature of human happiness and his argument is an enthymeme:

Happiness is said to be man's highest good because it is the attainment and enjoyment of the sovereign good.

In order to see that this is a valid syllogism, we need to supply the missing part before we can fully determine what the premises and conclusion are. Looking at the passage, we see that the first part makes a claim, "<u>happiness is said to be man's highest good</u>," and then a reason why the claim is true is given, "<u>because it is the attainment and enjoyment of the sovereign good</u>." This gives us a clue to what is missing, since premises are reasons for conclusions, the conclusion must be "<u>happiness is said to be man's highest good</u>." This leaves the rest as one of the premises. Thus, we have to supply the missing premise. So far we have:

All happiness is the attainment and enjoyment of the sovereign good.

<hr>

All happiness is said to be man's highest good.

To complete the syllogism we have to find a premise which would contain two of the three terms already used in such a way that the argument turns out to be valid:

All happiness is the attainment and enjoyment of the sovereign good.
Everything which is the attainment and enjoyment of the
sovereign good is said to be man's highest good.
All happiness is said to be man's highest good.

This can be schematized as:

All F is G.
All G is H.
All F is H.

A Venn diagram shows this to be a valid argument.

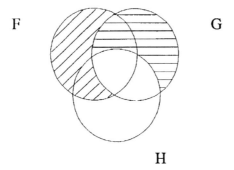

For each of the following arguments, write out the premises and conclusion in ordinary English sentences, create a schematic representation of its logical form, and then test its validity with a Venn diagram. Each of these arguments is an enthymeme and you will have to supply the missing part. [These arguments are based on ones actually used by the medieval theologian St. Thomas Aquinas.]

1.   Every body is potentiality different than it actually is. It is, then, impossible that God should be a body.

2.   No divine thing is subject to change, because all changeable things exist in time.

3.   Since all human souls are rational, no such soul is destroyed when the body dies.

§11 Complex Categorical Syllogisms

Not all argumentation is as simple as individual syllogisms. Sometimes we give complex arguments with many steps in support of our conclusions. When this is done with a series of syllogisms, the whole complex argument is call a **soritical argument**. Soritical arguments are chains of syllogisms which are interrelated. Such arguments can be interrelated in different ways, but the most common way is when the conclusion of one syllogism is used as one of the premises of the next syllogism and so on until the final conclusion (the conclusion of the whole soritical argument) is proved.

Because a soritical argument is an interconnected series of syllogisms, it must be composed of at least two smaller arguments. Thus, the way to analyze this kind of complex argument is to find the syllogisms which compose it. These syllogisms can then be analyzed in the usual way. Consider the following argument based on one by St. Thomas Aquinas:

Every human action is performed for the sake of some goal. In order to see that this is true, consider that all of those acts which are properly called "human" are those of which the person is the master. Therefore, all human acts are acts of reason and will. Now, because all human acts involve reason and will and every act which involves reason and will is performed with a deliberate act of choosing, it follows that all human acts are acts of choice. Now that we have shown that every truly human act is an act of choice, we can complete our argument. For in addition to this truth, it is also true that all acts of choice are directed at some goal. Consequently, all human acts must be directed at some goal.

By studying this argument, you will find that it is composed of three interconnected syllogisms:

All human acts are acts of which the person is master.
<u>All acts of which the person is master are acts of reason and will.</u>
All human acts are acts of reason and will.

All human acts are acts of reason and will.
<u>All acts of reason and will are acts of choice.</u>
All human acts are acts of choice.

All human acts are acts of choice.
<u>All acts of choice are directed at some goal.</u>
All human acts are directed at some goal.

These three syllogisms can be tested for validity with Venn diagrams in the usual way.

Read the following story and answer the questions which follow.

Sir Thomas Before the King

The king was tired and hungry. It was way past his supper time and this trial was becoming wearisome. Thus, it was with some temper that he greeted his minister and gave him leave to speak.

"Hail, Master Thomas," said the king, "let us have your evidence. But be mindful that I am weary, so none of your lawyer's wit now!"

Sir Thomas rose, bowed to the king and said, "Be at ease, Your Majesty, I shall be short. As to wit, my argument will only consist of three simple syllogisms."

"Well, on with it, man, the hour is late," ordered the king.

Thomas began, "Is it not true that every good king rules only by the will of God? I shall answer myself: indeed it is true. And anyone who rules by the will of God is responsible for the welfare of the kingdom. The conclusion is clear, good kings are responsible for the welfare of the kingdom. Now, if this is true and it is also true that no one responsible for the welfare of the state would knowingly allow corruption in his government, it follows that no good king would allow corruption in his government. But all toleration of evil ministers is an allowance of corruption in government. Therefore, Your Majesty, no good king will knowingly tolerate evil ministers."

In his present mood the king hardly appreciated this prick to his conscience, but he could not deny the logic of Sir Thomas' argument.

1. Does Sir Thomas present to the king a soritical argument?

    Yes __ No __

2. If you answered "no" to question 1, then explain what kind of argument he is giving and why the king thinks it is valid. If you answered "yes" to question 1, skip to the next question.

3. How many individual categorical syllogisms make up Sir Thomas' soritical argument?

    _____

4.   List the conclusions of each of the individual syllogisms in Sir Thomas' soritical argument.

_____

_____

_____

5.   Give a schematic representation of each of the individual syllogisms composing this soritical argument.

6.   Prove that Sir Thomas' whole argument is valid.

§12 Propositional Arguments

While Aristotle's syllogistic logic was used as the standard form of scientific reasoning up to modern times, ancient and medieval philosophers realized that the syllogism was not the only possible form of reasoning. In Aristotle's own time, another group of Greek philosophers, known as the Stoics, studied a different type of argument which we today call propositional argument. This kind of argument was developed by logicians of the Middle Ages and eventually became part of traditional logic. Unlike categorical syllogisms, the logical form (and so the validity) of propositional arguments does not depend on the distribution of terms within the propositions composing the argument, but on the arrangement of whole propositions within other more complex propositions which make up the argument.

Propositions can be used in two ways. When used categorically, the user asserts to be true what the proposition says. This is the kind of proposition used in categorical syllogisms which we have just studied. Propositions can also be used conditionally. When they are, the user does not assert as true what the proposition says. The proposition "Susan is attending Harvard and she will pay more tuition there" is categorical, because the speaker is asserting that what he says is true. On the other hand, the proposition "If Susan attends Harvard, she will pay more tuition" the speaker is not asserting that Susan is in fact attending Harvard nor that she is paying more tuition. The speaker is only saying that if it were true that Susan attended Harvard, a certain consequent would follow, namely that she would pay more tuition. Such "if . . . then" propositions are important, because we often want to say what would be true if a certain condition is met, even if that condition is never actually met or not now met.

Arguments which contain conditional propositions as premises are propositional arguments. They have a structure which is very different from categorical syllogisms. The most important difference is that the logical form of propositional arguments, as already noted, depends on the arrangement of propositions within complex propositions. All propositional arguments have at least one complex proposition among the premises. There are several different forms of propositional argument, some simple and some more complex. The first kind which we will study contain premises which are conditional propositions. It will, therefore, be necessary to say something more about conditional propositions.

Conditional Propositions

Consider the important difference between these two propositions:

[1] Master Giles is the logic master and I am unhappy.

[2] If Master Giles is the logic master, then I am unhappy.

Proposition [1] states something categorically--that is, without any conditions or qualifications. Proposition [2], on the other hand, does not state something categorically, but conditionally. In using [2] the speaker or writer is saying that a condition for his being unhappy is Master Giles being the logic master. If this condition is fulfilled, then it becomes true that he is unhappy. Notice that [2] can be true even when it is false that Master Giles is the logic master and false that I am unhappy. This is because the user of this proposition is not categorically saying that Master Giles is the logic master or that he is unhappy. He is only saying that if the condition is fulfilled (which it may not be) then there are certain consequences. In a conditional proposition, such as [2], one part states the condition and the other part says what will be true if the condition is fulfilled.

All conditional propositions are complex propositions, because they have parts which are themselves propositions. In [2] the part between the "if" and the "then" is the proposition "Master Giles is the logic master." The part following the "then" is the proposition "I am unhappy." We call the first proposition, the one which states the condition, the antecedent. We call the second proposition, the one which says what will be true on the condition that the antecedent is true, the consequent. Conditional propositions are usually expressed in English as "if . . . then" sentences. Other forms, however, can also occur, such as "when . . ." or "whenever . . ." or "on the condition that . . ." or "assuming that . . ." or some similar connecting phrase.

Hypothetical Syllogism

One of the forms of the categorical syllogism which we have studied is this pattern of argument:

[3]   All F is G.
        All G is H.
        All F is H.

An analogous type of argument using conditional propositions instead of categorical propositions is known as hypothetical syllogism:

[4]   If P then Q.
        If Q then R.
        If P then R.

In [4], the schematic letters P, Q, and R stand not for terms, but for whole propositions which are the parts composing the complex conditional propositions which are the premises and conclusion of the argument. This argument says, in effect, that if one thing (P) is the condition for another thing (Q) and that other thing (Q) is itself the condition for a third thing (R), then the first thing (P) must be the condition for the third thing (R). For example:

[5]   If Master Giles is the logic master, then I will be unhappy and if I am unhappy then I will do poorly at logic. Thus, if Master Giles is the logic master, I will do poorly at logic.

Hypothetical syllogism is a valid form of argument. Unlike the categorical syllogism [3], however, we cannot use a Venn diagram to prove its validity. This is, in fact, generally true of propositional arguments: we cannot test their validity with Venn diagrams. We just have to learn the valid forms and distinguish them from the invalid forms.

Modus Ponens

There are two very simple forms of propositional argument using conditional premises. Medieval logicians referred to the first of these by the Latin name "modus ponendo ponens." Today we call it "modus ponens" for short. In this kind of argument, there is a conditional premise and a second premise which is the antecedent of the conditional premise. We conclude to the consequent of the conditional premise. Thus, modus ponens follows the pattern:

[6]   If P then Q.
        P
        —————
        Q

We can see that this simple form of argument is valid by looking at an actual example:

[7]   If Master Giles is the logic master, I will be unhappy. Master Giles is indeed the logic master. Therefore, I am unhappy.

Modus ponens clearly shows what it means for one proposition to be a condition for another. The antecedent of the first premise states the condition and the consequent says what will be true if it is fulfilled. The second premise says that the condition stated in the antecedent is in fact fulfilled. In the conclusion the consequent is said to be true. This is clearly a valid form of argument, for it is impossible that the conclusion is false when all of the premises are true.

Modus Tollens

The other simple form of propositional argument using a conditional premise was the pattern to which medieval logicians gave the Latin name "modus tollendo tollens." Today we call it "modus tollens" for short. In this kind of argument, there is a conditional premise and a second premise which is the negation of the consequent of the conditional premise. We conclude to the negation of the antecedent of the conditional premise. Thus, modus tollens follows the pattern:

[8]   If P then Q.
        not-Q
        not-P

We can see that this simple form of argument is valid by looking at an actual example:

[9]   If Master Giles is the logic master, I will be unhappy. I am not unhappy. Therefore, Master Giles is not the logic master.

Modus tollens is clearly a valid form of argument, for on the assumption that the conditional proposition is really true and the consequent did not happen, it must be true that the condition stated in the antecedent was not fulfilled.

Disjunctive Syllogism

There are two other simple propositional arguments which do not make use of conditional premises. Each of them does make use of a distinctive type of complex proposition.

Sometimes in our reasoning we want to consider what is true or false with respect to some set of alternatives. The kind of proposition which states alternatives is called a disjunction. The most common way disjunctions are expressed in English is in "either . . . or" sentences. The following sentence, for example, expresses a disjunction:

[10]   Either Master Giles is the logic master or Master Hugh is.

It is clear from this example that disjunctions are complex propositions because they are composed of smaller propositions. In this example the smaller propositions are "Master Giles is the logic master" and "Master Hugh is the logic master." Each of these smaller propositions is called a "disjunct" of the whole disjunction. A disjunction is true if at least one of its disjuncts is true. Thus, [10] is true if either one of these masters is the logic master and, of course, it is true if both of them are. The only way that [10] can be false is if neither of them is the logic master.

Let us say that we know that a certain disjunction is true. Let us assume that we also know that one of its disjuncts is false. Then it must be the case that the other disjunct is true. This is disjunctive syllogism and follows the pattern of reasoning shown in the following schematic representation:

> [11] Either P or Q.
>   not P_____
>   Q

One premise of a disjunctive syllogism is a disjunction and the other premise is the negation of one of the disjuncts. The conclusion is the other disjunct. This kind of argument is clearly valid, because if the disjunctive premise is true then at least one of its disjuncts is true. So, if we know from the second premise that one of the disjuncts is false (because its negation is true) then it must be the other disjunct which accounts for the truth of the disjunctive premise. Thus, the following is a valid disjunctive syllogism:

[12]   Either Master Giles is the logic master or Master Hugh is. Master Hugh is not the logic master. Therefore, Master Giles must be.

Conjunctive Syllogism

A conjunction is a complex proposition made by joining two propositions with "and" or its equivalent. The smaller propositions composing the conjunction are called its "conjuncts." Conjunctions are true only when all conjuncts are true; otherwise they are false. Consider the following conjunction:

[13]   Both Master Giles and Master Hugh are demanding teachers.

This proposition is true only when it is true that Master Giles is a demanding teacher and it is also true that Master Hugh is a demanding teacher. If one of these conjuncts is false, then it cannot be the case that they are both true. If they are both false, of course, then their conjunction must also be false.

Let us say that we know that a certain conjunction is false (in other words, that its negation is true). Say we also know that one of the conjuncts is true. We can, then, conclude that the other conjunct must be false. The schematic representation of this kind of argument looks like this:

> [14] Not both P and Q.
>   P_____
>   not Q

Clearly this is a valid form of argument, because if we know that a conjunction is not true, then at least one of the conjuncts is false. Knowing that the one of the conjuncts is true leads us inevitability to the falsehood of the other conjunct. So, the following example is a valid conjunctive syllogism:

[15]   It is not the case that both Master Giles and Master Hugh are both logic masters. Master Hugh is the logic master. Thus, Master Giles cannot be.

Exercise 19   Student_____

For each of the following arguments, create a schematic representation showing its logical form and then identify the type of argument it is by giving its traditional name (one of the names used in §12).

1.   Either Brother Albert or Brother John will lecture on Aristotle's ethical treatise this year. It cannot be Brother John, because he has never read the treatise. Therefore, Brother Albert will give the lectures.

       argument name: _____

2.   If Brother Albert goes to Cologne to found a new school, then Brother Thomas will take his place on the theology faculty at the University of Paris. Albert is indeed going to Cologne where he will establish a new school. Thus, Brother Thomas is his successor on the theology faculty at Paris.

       argument name: _____

3.   When Brother Albert lectures on Aristotle, Brother Gerard always falls asleep. But Brother Gerard is awake! Brother Albert must not be lecturing on Aristotle.

       argument name: _____

4.   If Brother Albert establishes a school at Cologne, then there will, for the first time, be a school in Germany. If there is a school in Germany, then that country will be a better place to live. Clearly, when Brother Albert founds the new school at Cologne, Germany will be a better place to live.

       argument name: _____

5.   Whenever Brother Gerard is asked to attend a conference, he gets grumpy. The prior has just asked him to be present at the noon conference. Brother Gerard, then, is in a grumpy mood.

argument name: _____

6.   If Brother Thomas takes Brother Albert's place on the theology faculty at Paris, then he will be the youngest theologian there. We know that he is taking Albert's place, so he must indeed be the youngest theologian at the University of Paris.

argument name: _____

7.   Look, we know that it cannot be true that both Brother Albert and Brother John wrote this commentary on Aristotle's physical theories. We also know that Brother Albert is the only man here learned enough for such work. There can be no doubt that Brother John did not write the commentary.

argument name: _____

8.   I am afraid that you are mistaken about who wrote this commentary on Aristotle's physical theories. It must be Brother Albert. There are, after all, only two possibilities, Brother John did or Brother Albert did, and we know it is not Brother John.

argument name: _____

9. If the pope gives Brother Humbert the task of writing the book, then he will make Brother Albert bishop of Regensburg. If that happens, then Brother Albert will be the one to preach the Easter sermon. Therefore, if Brother Humbert is asked to write the book, Brother Albert will have to give the Easter sermon.

argument name: _____

10. I am certain that Brother Thomas will not arrive at the Council at Lyons. If he were to arrive, then he would have to be in good health now, but he is not.

argument name: _____

11. If I was a student of Brother Thomas at Saint-Jacques, I would have heard his brilliant lectures on the Book of Job, and I was. So, I heard his lectures.

argument name: _____

12. Master Roland either holds the professorship in theology for Frenchmen or for foreigners. But he cannot hold the professorship for Frenchmen, because he is from Cremona which is in Italy. The only other possibility is that he holds the professorship for foreigners.

argument name: _____

Read the following dialogue and answer the questions which follow.

On Human Nature

John Peckham: There exists two principles of life in man. One is his spiritual soul and the other is the animation of the body. That these are separate is affirmed by many ancient authorities, both Christian and pagan.

Thomas d'Aquino: I bow with respect for your great learning, Master John, for I am aware of your reputation as a scholar of ancient literature. Nonetheless, I find that I must disagree with your thesis that the principle of life in man is dual--one of the soul and the other of the body.

John Peckham: Thus, the debate is set, for either I am correct and there are two principles to human life or you are and there is but one. I submit that you cannot be correct about this most important issue and, therefore, I am correct that there are two principles of human life.

Thomas d'Aquino: Will you defend yourself by appealing to the authority of that most wise philosopher of the ancient Greeks, Plato?

John Peckham: Indeed I will, Master Thomas. It is recorded in the book of our holy father among the saints, the blessed Augustine, that Plato held that the soul is related to the body as a sailor to a ship. If Plato is correct about this--and I believe he is--then the body is the instrument of the soul. If the body is simply the instrument of the soul, then it is separate from the soul and completely distinct. Therefore, if Plato is correct, the body is a separate thing from the soul.

Thomas d'Aquino: Your argument is valid in form, Master John, but I wish to contend your premises. If Plato truly holds that the soul is related to the body as the sailor to the ship, then he believes that soul and body are related as mover and thing moved. You have just affirmed for us that Plato does use the sailor and ship as his analogy for the body and the soul. It clearly follows that Plato must hold that the soul and body are related as mover and moved thing.

John Peckham: You are correct, Plato is committed to that position.

Thomas d'Aquino: It cannot be that the soul is both the principle of the body and its separated mover, as you have just admitted Plato does. But you do agree that the soul is the principle of the body.

John Peckham: Yes, I do.

Thomas d'Aquino: Therefore, you must agree that Plato cannot be correct.

John Peckham: I see that I must concede your argument, Master Thomas.

1. Toward the beginning of the dialogue, Master John Peckham says that the debate is set and argues that he is correct and there are two principles of human life. What is the form of his argument? (Answer this by creating a schematic representation of the argument using any propositional letters you wish.)

2. What is the traditional name for Master John's argument?

    _____

3. Master John goes on to give an argument that if Plato is correct about the soul being related as a sailor and a ship then soul and body are separate. What is the form of his argument? (Answer this by creating a schematic representation of the argument using any propositional letters you wish.)

4. What is the traditional name for this argument of Master John?

    _____

5. What is the logical form of the argument which Master Thomas uses to prove that Plato must hold that the soul and body are related as mover and thing moved? (Answer this by creating a schematic representation of the argument using any propositional letters you wish.)

6.   What is the traditional name of Master Thomas' argument?

        _____

7.   What is the logical form of Master Thomas' final argument showing that the soul cannot
        be a separated mover?   (Answer this by creating a schematic representation of the
        argument using any propositional letters you wish.)

8.   What is the traditional name of Master Thomas' final argument?

        _____

§13 Facing Dilemmas

The propositional arguments we have studied so far are simple in their logical form. They are all arguments from two premises and represent a single step in the reasoning process. Not all of the arguments we use in everyday life are this simple, of course. Even some of our more complex arguments are made of these simpler arguments.

One such complex argument is traditionally called a dilemma. This very common sort of argument is often used when debating about human action and, so, often shows up in legal and moral argumentation. It always involves a set of alternatives--often alternative possible actions-- and concludes to what must be true or false given these alternatives. We have already seen that alternatives are stated in disjunctions. Thus, dilemmas will always have a disjunctive premise. There are two types of dilemma, each of which draws a conclusion from the alternatives in a different way.

Constructive Dilemma

Let us say that we know that either one of two things will happen. Say we further know that if the first happens a certain thing will result and that if the second thing happens the same thing will result. We can conclude that, no matter what, we will get our result. This sort of argument follows this pattern:

> [1] Either P or Q.
> If P then R.
> If Q then R.
> R

We can show that this complex form of argument is valid by showing that it can be reduced to the simpler, obviously valid, form of propositional argument we have just studied:

[1*]			
	(1)	Either P or Q.	first premise
	(2)	If P then R.	second premise
	(3)	If Q then R.	third premise
	(4)	P	first disjunct from (1)
	(5)	R	conclusion by modus ponens from (2) and (4)
	(6)	Q	second disjunct from (1)
	(7)	R	conclusion by modus ponens from (3) and (6)
	(8)	R	conclusion from (1), (2), and (3)

This argument draws the conclusion R, no matter which of the two possibilities P and Q is true. The arguer believes that the disjunctive premise is true and so knows that at least one of the disjuncts P and Q is true. So, at lines (4) and (6) he takes each of the alternatives in turn and shows that each separately leads to R by a modus ponens argument. Thus, a constructive dilemma is a complex argument composed of simpler modus ponens arguments. Compare the schematic representation in [1] to the following example:

[2]   Either Master Giles will be the logic master or Master Hugh will. If Master Giles is, then I will have a difficult term. If Master Hugh is, then I will still have a difficult term. Thus, no matter which is the logic master, I will have a difficult term.

Destructive Dilemma

Let us say that we know that either one of two things will not happen. Say we further know that a certain thing will make the first alternative happen and that very same thing will also make the second thing happen. We can conclude that, no matter what, that certain thing will not occur. This sort of argument follows this pattern:

[3]   Either not-P or not-Q.
        If R then P.
        If R then Q._____
        not-R

We can show that this complex form of argument is valid by showing that it can be reduced to the simpler, obviously valid, form of propositional argument we have just studied:

[3*]   (1) Either not-P or not-Q.   first premise
        (2) If R then P.   second premise
        (3) If R then Q.   third premise
        (4) not-P   first disjunct from (1)
        (5) not-R   conclusion by modus tollens from (2) and (4)
        (6) not-Q   second disjunct from (1)
        (7) not-R   conclusion by modus tollens from (3) and (6)
        (8) not-R   conclusion from (1), (2), and (3)

This argument draws that conclusion that R is false, no matter which of the two possibilities P and Q is false. The arguer believes that the disjunctive premise is true and so knows that at least one of the disjuncts P and Q is false. So, at lines (4) and (6) he takes each of the alternatives in turn and shows that each separately leads to not-R by a modus tollens argument. Thus, destructive dilemma is a complex argument composed of simpler modus tollens arguments. Compare the schematic representation in [3] to the following example:

[4] Neither Master Giles nor Master Hugh will be the logic master. But whenever Master Gilbert is ill, then both Master Giles and Master Hugh are logic masters. Thus, it cannot be true that Master Gilbert is ill.

In analyzing a dilemma, you should at least be able to recognize the set of alternatives presented in the premises and state them clearly in the form of a disjunction. You should also be able to state clearly the conditional propositions which connect the alternatives with a certain result and you should be able to recognize and state clearly the conclusion. You can show that you understand precisely how the dilemma works if you can go beyond this to explaining, as in [1*] and [3*], what simpler types of propositional reasoning lead us from the premises to the conclusion.

Read the following story and answer the questions which follow.

In Vino Veritas?

Two young men, both students at the university, were walking home from the tavern through the narrow streets of medieval Paris. Though their steps were somewhat unsteady, they felt their minds as sharp as ever.

One said to the other, "Do you believe that in wine there is truth?"

"Why, of course," replied the other. "Did not some ancient poet say as much?"

"Well, then, since we have drunk a good deal of wine this evening, it is a good time to do some philosophy. So, let us together seek the truth about human nature."

"In that case," said the second young man, "we should begin with a definition. It is clear to me that man should be defined as the only featherless biped."

"You fool!" exclaimed his companion. "What kind of a definition is that?"

"A true one," said the other, lifting his chin in a gesture of intellectual pride.

"As we are philosophers, sir, you must be ready to defend your claim with argument!" challenged the first young man.

"Then I shall. Consider this, you doubter: either every biped other than man has feathers or every unfeathered creature other than man has more than two legs. These are the only possibilities and no matter which is true, my definition holds. Refute that, if you can!"

The first young man, saying nothing, jumped over a nearby low wall. The second stood in the street, not knowing what to make of his companion's strange behavior. Then suddenly, with a loud screech, something white flew over the wall and landed at the second man's feet. It was a plucked chicken.

1.   Reconstruct the second young man's argument for his definition of a human being by writing out in clear English sentences each of his premises and his conclusion.

   Premises: _____

   _____

   _____

   Conclusion: _____

   _____

2.   What is the traditional name for an argument of this form?

      _____

3.   Did the first young man refute the second's argument? Why or why not?

      Yes ___   No ___

      _____

      _____

      _____

      _____

§14 Arguments to Absurdity

One of the most common types of argument is indirect proof which is often called by its medieval Latin name "reductio ad absurdum." In this type of argument one tries to prove a certain conclusion by disproving its negation. Because, for every proposition, either it or its negation is true, by disproving the negation of a certain proposition one has in fact proved the proposition itself. A proposition can be disproved by showing that it logically leads to absurd results. Contradictions are always logically absurd, because they are always false. For example:

Master Giles both is and is not the logic master.

In fact, any complex proposition of the form "P and not-P" is always false. Any proposition from which a contradiction like this can be deduced must also be false, which means that its negation is true. Thus, one can prove a certain proposition if one can show that its negation leads to a contradiction. This is a reductio ad absurdum argument and has the form:

To prove a proposition P:

Assume that its negation not-P is true
(for the sake of argument).

Show that not-P leads to a contradiction
(any proposition of the form Q and not-Q, where Q is any proposition).

If not-P leads to absurd results, then it cannot be true and if not-P cannot be true then P must be true (because either P or not-P, for any proposition P).

Therefore, P.

A famous example of a reductio ad absurdum argument from the history of philosophy is Descartes' cogito ergo sum (I think therefore I am) argument. It goes something like this:

Do I exist? Well, let's say that I don't, just for the sake of argument. Now, if I say that I don't exist, then I doubt my existence. But in order to doubt my existence I must exist. So, on the assumption that I don't exist, I both exist and I don't exist! This, of course, is impossible. Therefore, I must exist.

Descartes wants to prove that he exists. In order to do this he assumes that he does not exist. He makes this assumption, not because he believes it is true, but because he wants to show that it is not true. If he can show this, then he will have shown that he must exist. (This is because if "I do not exist" cannot be true, then "I do exist" must be true.) So, how does he show that "I do not exist" cannot be true? He shows that a contradiction follows from it. In other words, he shows that if he accepts "I do not exist" as true, then he must also accept "I both exist and I don't exist" as true. But he cannot accept this second proposition as true, because it is a contradiction. So, he cannot accept "I do not exist" as true either.

A reductio ad absurdum (reduction to impossibility) argument is a very powerful form of reasoning. By means of it one can prove indirectly (by disproving a certain proposition) that a conclusion (the disproved proposition's negation) must be true without actually showing that anything directly leads us to that conclusion.

Consider the following example, which is one version of the famous argument from design for the existence of God:

The order evident in the universe shows that God must exist. If this were not so, then the observed order must have been the result of absolutely random processes. But if this is true, then the universe would be unintelligible. But the universe clearly is intelligible as modern science shows. Therefore, God, the creator of the universe, must exist.

If this argument is broken down into its separate steps of reasoning, it becomes clear how the contradiction is derived from the premise assumed for the sake of argument.

1.	God does not exist	assumption made for the sake of argument (premise)
2.	If God does not exist, then universe is random.	assumption (premise)
3.	If universe is random, then it is unintelligible.	assumption (premise)
4.	Universe is intelligible.	assumption (premise)
5.	Universe is random.	1, 2 modus ponens
6.	Universe is unintelligible.	3, 5 modus ponens
7.	Universe is intelligible and it's unintelligible.	4, 6 conjunction
8.	God exists.	1, 7 conclusion drawn by reductio ad absurdum

The question between us is whether God exists. You and I agree that 2 and 3 are true. We also agree that 4 is true, because we both think that modern science can tell us a lot about the world. I show you, then, that if you assume that you are right that God doesn't exist, then that leads to a contradiction by steps 5-7. Since we agreed that our assumptions 2, 3, and 4 are correct and we don't want to give them up, we have to admit that 1 cannot be true since, along with the assumptions 2, 3, and 4 it leads to a contradiction. Thus, we have to accept the conclusion at 8.

Read the following dialogue and answer the questions which follow.

On Certain Knowledge

Brother Peter:	Master Albert, will you answer a question for me?
Brother Albert:	Most certainly, Brother Peter, if I am able.
Brother Peter:	I was today reading in a book of the ancient writer Cicero, who is revered as a very wise man by many.
Brother Albert:	You may be sure that I am among the many who hold the learned Cicero in great esteem.
Brother Peter:	He says in his book that, in his day, there were philosophers called "skeptics" who claimed that no man should ever say that he knows anything with certainty.
Brother Albert:	Does Cicero say why these skeptics held this position?
Brother Peter:	Yes, he says they argued that if a man can always be wrong in his beliefs, then he can never be certain in his beliefs. It is clear that we imperfect mortal men are always liable to error. Therefore, we can never be certain about anything we believe.
Brother Albert:	I suppose these skeptics go on to argue that, given this and the proposition that if we can never be certain about any of our beliefs, then we ought never to say that we know anything with certainty, their injunction never to claim certainty follows.
Brother Peter:	That is correct, Master.
Brother Albert:	Tell me, Brother, are you inclined to accept this conclusion?
Brother Peter:	I am, for it seems proper to man to humbly admit his limitations.
Brother Albert:	Far be it from me to deny the value of humility. Nonetheless, perhaps we can find a logical flaw in the position of the skeptics.
Brother Peter:	What do you mean, Master Albert?

Brother Albert:	Let us accept, for the moment, that the skeptics' claim is true. If it is, then they know it with certainty. After all, if they assert it to be true, it is because they know it to be true with certainty.
Brother Peter:	Yes, I do think that they claimed to know with certainty that they are correct.
Brother Albert:	Now, if they knew it with certainty, then they had no doubt.
Brother Peter:	Yes.
Brother Albert:	In other words, they knew it with certainty.
Brother Peter:	Yes, that is correct.
Brother Albert:	But their claim is that nobody ever knows anything with certainty.
Brother Peter:	Yes.
Brother Albert:	It follows, then, that the skeptics both know the truth of their claim with certainty and do not know the truth of their claim with certainty.
Brother Peter:	But that is impossible!
Brother Albert:	It is indeed. Thus, the skeptics cannot be correct that man can never know anything with certainty and this is proved by the very claim that they make.

1. Brother Peter relates the skeptics' argument that human beings can never know anything with certainty. What is the skeptics' argument?

Premises: _____

_____

_____

_____

Conclusion: _____

_____

2.	What is the traditional name for this kind of argument?

	_____

3.	Brother Albert goes on to complete the skeptics' argument, explaining how they arrived at the conclusion that no one should ever claim to know anything for sure. What are the premises of the argument which lead to this conclusion?

	Premises: _____

	_____

	_____

	_____

4.	What kind of argument does Brother Albert use to refute the skeptics?

	_____

5.	When Brother Albert says "Let us accept, for the moment, that the skeptics' claim is true" does he say this because he really thinks it is true?

	Yes __	No __

6.	If you answered "yes" to question 5, explain how Albert can believe the skeptics are correct and still refute them. If you answered "no" then skip to question 7.

	_____

	_____

	_____

	_____

7. Explain why Brother Albert suggests that he and Brother Peter accept the claim.

_____

_____

_____

_____

8. Write out all the premises of Brother Albert's argument refuting the skeptics.

   Premises: _____

   _____

   _____

   _____

9. When Brother Peter says "that is impossible" what is the proposition that he cannot accept?

   _____

   _____

10. Why can't Peter accept this proposition?

   _____

   _____

11. How can Brother Albert be certain that his conclusion about the falsity of the skeptics' claim is true?

   _____

   _____

   _____

Student: _____

Read the following dialogue and answer the questions which follow.

On the Largest Prime Number

Brother Ulrich:	Brother Albert, come walk with me in the cloisters, I have a mathematical question I would like to ask you.
Brother Albert:	No other discipline keeps the mind sharp as does mathematics. Yes, let us walk.
Brother Ulrich:	I have been reading your fine commentary on Euclid's <u>Elements of Geometry</u>. You explain many things very well. Nonetheless, I find that I do not fully understand one particular argument of Euclid which you discuss.
Brother Albert:	To which of Euclid's many arguments do you refer, Brother?
Brother Ulrich:	It is the famous argument in which he demonstrates that there cannot be a largest prime number. How can he establish such a conclusion? After all, he cannot directly test every possible number to determine whether or not it is prime, for there is an infinity of numbers.
Brother Albert:	You are correct, one cannot consider individually every element in an infinite series.
Brother Ulrich:	How, then, does Euclid prove something concerning the infinite series of numbers?
Brother Albert:	You will recall, from what you read, that he first assumes that there is a largest prime number.
Brother Ulrich:	Yes, I do remember this and I was and remain confused by it. Why does he assume what he believes to be false?
Brother Albert:	We do not always assert propositions as true. Sometimes we use a proposition in argument even though we know it to be false. Perhaps you will understand how we can do this by following closely Euclid's argument.
Brother Ulrich:	Yes, let us review the argument step by step.

Brother Albert:	As I said, Euclid begins by assuming that there exists a largest prime number. Let us agree to designate this number, whatever it is, by the letter K.
Brother Ulrich:	So, K is the largest prime number.
Brother Albert:	Yes. Now, let us define another number, call it N, to be the number obtained by multiplying together all prime numbers less than or equal to K.
Brother Ulrich:	Thus, we now have two numbers: K, which we assume is the largest prime, and N, which is the product of all the primes less than or equal to K.
Brother Albert:	Let us now add 1 to the number N. It is clear that N + 1 is larger than K.
Brother Ulrich:	Yes, that is clear.
Brother Albert:	It is also clear that N + 1 is a prime number, because it leaves a remainder of 1 when divided by any of the prime numbers less than or equal to K.
Brother Ulrich:	Yes, that is true.
Brother Albert:	But if N + 1 is prime and is larger than K, as we have just seen it is, then we have a contradiction, do we not?
Brother Ulrich:	We do indeed, Brother Albert. For we have just proved that K is the largest prime number and that K is not the largest prime number. This is, of course, impossible.
Brother Albert:	We reached this absurd conclusion by assuming that there is some number K which is the largest prime.
Brother Ulrich:	Yes, we did.
Brother Albert:	Clearly, we must now reject this assumption, for we have proved that it leads to impossible results.
Brother Ulrich:	Our assumption, then, must be false.
Brother Albert:	If the assumption that there is a largest prime number must be false, then what must be true?

Brother Ulrich: Clearly, that there is no largest prime number.

Brother Albert: Now, Brother Ulrich, you see how something can be proved of an infinite series without investigating each member of the series.

1. What type of argument does Euclid use to prove that there is no largest prime number? (Give the traditional name for this kind of argument.)

    _____

2. Euclid's argument is intended to demonstrate that there is no largest prime number, so why does he begin by assuming that there is a largest prime number?

    _____

    _____

    _____

3. What are the premises of Euclid's argument? (Number each of the premises.)

    _____

    _____

    _____

    _____

4. What is the conclusion of Euclid's argument?

    _____

    _____

5. What is the logical form of Euclid's argument? (Create a schematic representation of the argument with as much detail as possible.)

Exercise 24   Student: _____

Read the following dialogue and answer the questions which follow.

On the Sphericity of the Earth

Young Scholar:	Is this the Convent of Saint-Jacques?
Brother Albert:	Yes it is, young man. What is it you seek?
Young Scholar:	I was told that I might find here a certain Master Albert of Cologne. Do you know of this learned man?
Brother Albert:	Of the man, I do indeed know him to the extent that any of us know ourselves. As for learning, I will leave that for God and posterity to decide.
Young Scholar:	So, you are Albert of Cologne?
Brother Albert:	Yes, you have found the one you seek.
Young Scholar:	God be with you, Master. May I have a word with you?
Brother Albert:	You look as though you have traveled far. Come into the refectory and have a cup of wine. We can talk there.
Young Scholar:	[sitting before a cup of wine] I have indeed traveled far. I am from the island of Sicily and I have come here to Paris to study at the university. My Latin master back home told me that Paris is the City of the Philosophers and ever since I was a boy, I have wanted to come here to study.
Brother Albert:	So, you wish to be a philosopher?
Young Scholar:	Yes, and that is why I have come to see you. I have heard that you know well the books of the great Aristotle, who is the father of those who know. I wish to know from a man who is learned in the science of Aristotle, such as yourself, whether I am fit to study philosophy or whether I should return home and take up some trade.
Brother Albert:	I see. If we, perhaps, investigate some scientific question together, we may know which of these vocations you should pursue.

Young Scholar:	I would be pleased, Master, if we could do this.
Brother Albert:	Besides your Latin, what subjects have you studied?
Young Scholar:	Geometry and astronomy.
Brother Albert:	Let us, then, consider an astronomical question. Tell me, what is the shape of the earth?
Young Scholar:	The earth is a sphere.
Brother Albert:	Good. Now, why are we able to say this with certainty?
Young Scholar:	It seems to me that there are two possibilities. The first is that we know it by sense perception, as we could if we were able to move off the surface of the earth far enough to see it as a whole. The second is that we know it by argument, as we could beginning with what our senses tell us is true and reasoning to the necessity of the earth's sphericity. Either way we would know that the earth must be a sphere.
Brother Albert:	Very good, young man! Your argument presents us with a clear picture of our task. You are correct to identify these two alternatives as the only possible means for knowing the earth to be spherical. It remains for us to see which of them is truly possible for us. Let us begin with your first alternative. Is it possible for man to remove himself from the earth's surface far enough to see the whole earth all at once?
Young Scholar:	Not until man learns to fly.
Brother Albert:	True. But, let us assume that man invents a device to lift him from the surface of the earth many miles. In such a case would he able to see enough of the earth to say, from visual perception alone, that the earth is a sphere?
Young Scholar:	I see your point, Master. No man could ever be in a position to view the whole earth at once. Any position he took would only show him one surface of the earth at a time appearing to him as a disk. So, even with a flying device, man cannot know that the earth is a sphere from sense perception alone.
Brother Albert:	Good. Your argument is a valid syllogism. Can you restate it so that we may see its form more clearly?

Young Scholar:	I think I can. Any position a man can take with respect to the earth will only allow him to see one surface of the earth. No man who sees only one surface of the earth knows from visual perception alone that the earth is a sphere. Therefore, no position a man can take with respect to the earth allows him to know from visual perception alone that the earth is a sphere.
Brother Albert:	This leaves us with the other alternative, namely, that we know that the earth is a sphere by argument.
Young Scholar:	Yes, Master.
Brother Albert:	So, is there anything we know about the nature of the earth which might lead us to conclude that it must be a sphere?
Young Scholar:	Perhaps, something about how objects on the surface of the earth move with respect to the earth.
Brother Albert:	An excellent suggestion! What sort of motion is characteristic of objects on or near the surface of the earth?
Young Scholar:	Well, there is motion perpendicular to the earth's surface.
Brother Albert:	Good. Now, what sort of object moves perpendicularly to the surface of the earth?
Young Scholar:	Falling objects.
Brother Albert:	True. It is important that this is motion that is in accord with the nature of the earth, for if it is not, then we learn nothing essential about the earth itself. So, is the free fall of objects near the surface of the earth natural?
Young Scholar:	Yes.
Brother Albert:	How do we know this is true?
Young Scholar:	We know that it is true, because its denial leads to contradiction.
Brother Albert:	Good. Now, set out the argument that demonstrates this.
Young Scholar:	Let us assume that falling motion is not natural. If this is true, then it proceeds from an external source and not an internal source. In free fall, nothing external is acting on the falling object, so it is a natural motion. But we assumed that falling motion was not natural. Therefore, objects free falling toward the center of the earth are moving naturally.

Brother Albert:	Very good. Now, we are in a position to complete our argument. We can certainly accept the premise that the earth is a physical body to which freely falling objects gravitate perpendicularly over its entire surface.
Young Scholar:	Yes, we can.
Brother Albert:	Further, we know that any body to which falling objects gravitate in this way must be spherical. Please state the conclusion.
Young Scholar:	The earth is spherical.
Brother Albert:	I think, young man, that you must not return to Sicily, but remain here and become a citizen of the City of the Philosophers.

1.   What form of argument does the Young Scholar use to show that it is possible to be certain that the earth is a sphere?

        _____

2.   What are the three premises of this argument? (Write out the premises in ordinary English sentences.)

        Premise 1: _____

        _____

        Premise 2: _____

        _____

        Premise 3: _____

        _____

3.   Is the Young Scholar's argument valid?

        Yes __ No __

4.	What is the logical form of the categorical syllogism which the Young Scholar uses to establish that no one can ever be in a position to observe enough of the earth to see that it must be a sphere? (Give a schematic representation of the argument using any schematic letters you wish.)

5.	Prove that Brother Albert is correct to say that the Young Scholar's syllogism is valid.

6.	What is the argument which convinces Brother Albert that he and the Young Scholar can only prove that the earth is a sphere by means of argument? (Write out the premises and the conclusion.)

	Premises: _____

	_____

	Conclusion: _____

	_____

7.	What kind of argument is this? (Give its traditional name.)

	_____

8.	What kind of argument does the Young Scholar give to show that gravitational motion must be natural? (Give the traditional name.)

	_____

9.   What is the proposition the Young Scholar is trying to disprove with this argument?

_____

10.   What is the contradiction which disproves this proposition?

_____

_____

11.   What is the logical form of the argument that Brother Albert uses to finally prove that the earth is spherical? (Give a schematic representation of the argument.)

12.   Is the argument valid? (Use a Venn diagram to answer this question.)

valid/invalid

§15 Induction

All of the various types of argument we have studied so far are types of deductive argument. Deductive arguments are those which attempt to show that, given the premises, the conclusion is absolutely necessary. As we have seen, when this kind of argument is valid, it is impossible that the conclusion is false when all of the premises are true. So, deductive argument is the strongest type of argument, because it shows that the conclusion is necessarily linked with the premises. In other words, the conclusion follows from the premises in such a way that it cannot be otherwise.

Not all of our arguments, however, are this strict. Sometimes the best we can do is to show that certain premises make a particular conclusion likely, even though they do not absolutely necessitate it. This less strict sort of argument is call inductive argument. When a person argues with an inductive argument, he is not saying that the conclusion <u>must</u> be true when all of the premises are true. He is saying that the premises provide some degree of evidence which makes the conclusion <u>probably</u> true. Thus, it is possible that, in a good inductive argument, the premises are all true and the conclusion is still false. This, of course, could not be the case in a valid deductive argument. The basic difference between deductive and inductive arguments is the kind of claim each is making. Deductive arguments claim that the conclusion must be true when the premises are true while inductive arguments claim that the conclusion is probably true when the premises are true.

One of the most common types of inductive reasoning is an argument which attempts to draw a universal conclusion from premises concerning individuals. This often happens in the natural sciences. A zoologist, for example, might conclude that the Egyptian goose always builds its nests over water on the basis of a series of observations of the nesting behavior of individual geese. Thus, his argument works like this:

The first nesting Egyptian goose I observed built her nest over water.

The second nesting Egyptian goose I observed built her nest over water.

The third nesting Egyptian goose I observed built her nest over water.

The Nth (where N is some number) nesting Egyptian goose I observed built her nest over water.

Therefore, every nesting Egyptian goose I will ever observe will build her nest over water.

The claim that the arguer is making here is that his observation of so many cases of Egyptian goose nesting behavior is enough to allow him to conclude correctly that this behavior is typical of the species. Of course, strictly speaking, it is always possible that tomorrow he will observe an Egyptian goose building a nest over dry land. So, there is no absolutely necessary connection between his observations to date and his conclusion. But chances are good that what he has observed a sufficiently large number of geese do is what they all do.

The question which arises with inductive argument is whether the premises provide enough evidence for the conclusion. In the case of our example above, has the zoologist observed enough cases to draw his universal conclusion? How many cases are enough to allow him to draw this conclusion?

Medieval natural philosophers were the first to attempt a systematic answer to these questions. They were concerned to discover inductive methods which were reliable enough to allow the natural scientist to determine the causes of natural phenomena. They distinguished three types of induction.

Simple Enumeration

Induction by simple enumeration is similar to the type used in the example of the Egyptian goose just discussed. In this type of inductive argument, the scientist attempts to learn the cause of a certain effect by simply counting the cases where the effect is preceded by the suspected cause. If, after looking at many cases, the scientist has never observed the effect without this cause, he then draws the conclusion that this is indeed the true cause of the effect. The following illustrates this method:

Case	Circumstances	Effect
1	P	E
2	P	E
3	P	E
4	P	E

Therefore, P is the cause of E.

When one induces by simple enumeration, one is saying that, because an effect E is always or typically preceded by circumstance P in every case studied, the two are causally related. Of course, the more cases one investigates in this kind of induction, the stronger the conclusion. Even so, simple enumeration is the weakest form of induction, for we can never guarantee that the very next case we investigate will be like all the earlier cases. Somewhat stronger types of induction are the methods of agreement and difference.

Method of Agreement

When a scientist observes something happening, he wants to know why it is happening. In asking "why?" the scientist is seeking the cause for what he observes. One way of using inductive argument to determine the cause for a certain effect is the method of agreement. The scientist observes the effect occurring on a number of occasions. Each time he takes careful note of the circumstances surrounding the occurrence of the effect. Say he notes that, while some of the circumstances vary (are present in some cases of the effect but not on others), some are always there. When this happens, then he has good reason to conclude that the circumstances which are always present are causally related to the effect he is studying. This might be illustrated by the following chart:

Case	Circumstances	Effect
1	PQRS	E
2	PRT	E
3	PQTU	E
4	PSU	E

Therefore, P is the cause of E.

Notice that, although the circumstances in which the effect E occurs change, one element of the circumstances is always present, namely P. The scientist, then, is justified in drawing the conclusion that P is the cause of (or at least part of the cause of) E. As with all types of induction, the method of agreement does not prove with absolute necessity that P is the cause of E, but only that it is probably the cause.

Method of Difference

Another way of using inductive argument to find the cause of something is to look for differences in what happens in changing circumstances. This can be done by comparing two cases, one where the effect occurs and one where it does not. If it can be shown that a certain circumstance or set of circumstances is present when the effect occurs and absent when the effect does not occur, then one can inductively conclude that this circumstance or set of circumstances is causally related to the effect. This method can be illustrated by the following:

Case	Circumstances	Effect
1	PQR	E
2	QR	

Therefore, P is the cause of E.

Notice that the effect E occurs only when P is present. This is grounds for claiming that P has something to do with why E happens. This kind of argument does not show that P is absolutely necessary for E, but it does make it probable that P is required for E to happen.

Read the following arguments and determine whether they are inductive or deductive. If the argument is inductive, then specify the type of induction used. If the argument is deductive, then specify the type of deduction by giving its traditional name.

1.   Brother Dietrich, the monastery pharmacist, was testing the effect of a certain herb on the taste. He administered it to five monks. All five complained that it tasted bitter and one said that, in addition, it had a dry aftertaste. Four of the monks were in good health when they tasted the herb and one had a fever. Three of the monks tasted the herb in the morning before they had anything to eat, a fourth tasted it after eating his breakfast oatmeal and the fifth tasted it after drinking some wine. Brother Dietrich concluded that the herb was indeed a bitter herb.

-----

2.   One morning the abbot noticed a young novice throwing a stone over the courtyard wall. Approaching him the abbot said, "Certainly you have something better to do with your time, Brother. Besides, throwing stones over the wall like this may result in injury to someone on the other side." "I am certain that I will not hurt anyone on the other side, Reverand Abbot," said the young man. "How can you be so certain?" asked the abbot. The novice replied, "I have been throwing stones over this wall at this time every day for the past nine months and I have never once hurt anyone."

-----

3.   Brother James' workshop was a fascinating place and Brother Stephen liked to stop there on his way to evening prayer. "What are you working on today, Brother?" asked Stephen. "I have been working on a way of making our reed paper stronger," replied James. James went on to explain that he had just succeeded in making the monastery's reed paper twice as strong as before. But Brother Stephen was skeptical and asked how James could be so sure that his paper was twice as strong as the paper they had been using. James replied, "Up to now, we have been making our paper with the fibers all running the same say. I have found a way in which I can layer the sheets so that the fibers of one layer are running at right angles to those of the other layer. Now, we know that if the fibers of the paper cross each other at right angles, it takes twice as much effort to pull them apart. We also know that if it takes twice as much effort to pull the fibers apart, then the paper is twice as strong. This is why I know that my new paper is twice as strong as our old paper."

-----

4.   One day, while visiting the emperor's aviary, Brother Albert took advantage of the opportunity to test a story which he often read in the books of animal lore. The story says that the ostrich can eat and digest iron. Albert was doubtful, but thought that it was worth a test. He offered some small pieces of iron to the three ostriches in the aviary every day for several consecutive days. None of the ostriches showed any interest in the iron. He concluded that the story was probably just a legend.

---

5.   Brother Albert was discussing infectious diseases of horses with the emperor's stable master. He asked the stable master the circumstances under which the disease spread through the stables. The stable master told him that he had observed three different situations in which a healthy horse became ill. The first was when an infected horse bit a healthy horse which then became ill. This happened at least three times. The second was when an infected horse urinated near its stable-mate which then became ill. There was one case of this occurrence. The third was when an infected horse would leave a corrupted discharge on a post or similar object which would then come into contact with healthy horses which then became ill. There were five cases of this in all. Brother Albert, then, noted that the common element in each of these cases is that a healthy horse came into contact with bodily fluids of an infected horse such as urine, blood, saliva, or drainage from wounds. He drew the conclusion that these fluids were the vehicle of the infection's spread.

---

6.   Brother Dietrich suspected that the herb he used to treat nausea was effective only if its medicinal properties were released by boiling. He give the three monks in the infirmary suffering from nausea equal doses of the herb. He had the first consume the herb uncooked and noted that his nausea was not relieved. He had the second consume the herb after it had been boiled for five minutes and the third drink a tea made from the herb. The second and third monks reported some relief from their nausea and Brother Deitrich knew that his suspicion was confirmed.

---

§16 Formal Fallacies

A fallacy is a logical mistake. We have already seen that we make a logical mistake whenever we try to prove a conclusion by means of an invalid argument. In such a case we think or say something is proved when it really is not proved. These kinds of fallacies are called formal fallacies, because they are mistakes concerning the form of arguments. Anytime we think that an argument has a valid form when it really does not, we commit a formal fallacy. Thus, anyone who argues for a conclusion by means of a categorical syllogism whose Venn diagram shows it to be invalid commits a formal fallacy. Two common formal fallacies involving propositional arguments are often mistaken for modus ponens and modus tollens. These are treated in what follows.

Affirming the Consequent

Consider an argument with a conditional proposition and its consequent as premises which draws the antecedent of the conditional as its conclusion. Such an argument looks something like modus ponens, but in fact it is a different fallacious argument known as affirming the consequent. Its logical form is:

> If P then Q.
> $\underline{Q\qquad\qquad}$
> P

For example: If Brother Joseph fails to learn logic, then Master Giles will be disappointed in him. Master Giles is disappointed in Brother Joseph. Thus, Brother Joseph has failed to learn logic.

This is clearly invalid, because the conclusion might be false even if the premises are true. That is, the truth of both premises does not make absolutely necessary the truth of the conclusion, for Brother Joseph might not have failed logic while Master Giles is disappointed in him for other reasons.

Denying the Antecedent

Consider an argument with a conditional proposition and the negation of its antecedent as premises which draws the negation of its consequent as a conclusion. Such an argument looks something like modus tollens, but in fact it is a different fallacious argument known as denying the antecedent. Its logical form is:

> If P then Q.
> not P
> _____
> not Q

For example: If Brother Joseph fails to learn logic, then Master Giles will be disappointed in him. Brother Joseph has not failed to learn logic. Therefore, Master Giles is not disapppointed in him.

This argument is also invalid, for again the premises do not necessitate the conclusion. It might be that Master Giles is still disappointed in Brother Joseph even though he learned logic.

Formal fallacies are not the only kind of logical mistake. Some fallacies are informal and concern mistakes such as thinking something is true when it is really false, making connections between things which really do not go together, saying that there are only two (or three, or four, etc.) choices when there are really many more, and others. These are the kinds of mistakes fall into various categories are treated in the sections which follow.

Consider the following arguments. If they are valid, give the traditional name of this type of reasoning. If they are invalid, give the traditonal name of this type of fallacy.

1.   If Brother Thomas gives a formal lecture on the soul, he will criticize Plato's views on the unity of the human person. Brother Thomas criticized Plato's views on the unity of the person. Therefore, he must have given a formal lecture.

       _____

2.   If Brother Thomas studied with Brother Albert at Cologne, then he must have first read Aristotle's book on ethics there. He did study with Albert at the new Dominican school at Cologne. Therefore, he certainly read Aristotle's book on ethics for the first time at Cologne.

       _____

3.   If Brother Thomas studied with Brother Albert at Cologne, then he must have first read Aristotle's book on ethics there. But he first read Aristotle's book on ethics at Naples, not Cologne. Therefore, he cannot have studied with Albert at Cologne.

       _____

4.   If Brother Thomas studied with Brother Albert at Cologne, then he must have first read Aristotle's book on ethics there. Brother Thomas did not study with Albert at Cologne and, therefore, did not first read Aristotle's <u>Ethics</u> there.

       _____

5.   If Brother Thomas is sent to Saint-Jacques, then he will certainly be appointed to the professorship in theology at the university. He was just appointed a professor of theology. Therefore, he must have been sent to live at Saint-Jacques.

       _____

§17 Fallacies of Ambiguity

Often we make mistakes in our reasoning because we are unclear in our use of words. This ambiguity can effect the validity of our arguments by allowing for different possible interpretations of the words that compose the propositions and terms of the arguments. Thus, words are ambiguous when they can be understood in more than one way. Ambiguity can show up in our propositions in different ways and for different reasons. Three of the more important fallacies of ambiguity are introduced in what follows.

Fallacy of Equivocation

One of the most important of the fallacies of ambiguity is the fallacy of equivocation. It is essential in an argument that the meaning of the terms remains constant. If someone changes the meaning of a term in the middle of the argument, it might look as if it is valid when it really is not. For example, consider the following syllogism:

All criminal actions are illegal acts and all prosecutions for theft are criminal actions. Therefore, all prosecutions for theft are illegal acts.

Here the arguer has changed the meaning of the term "criminal actions." In the first premise it means "the action of criminals when committing a crime" and in the second premise it means "legal proceedings against criminals." Thus, this syllogism has four distinct terms and not three terms, as it might appear. In this case the mistake the arguer has made is that he has equivocated on the term "criminal actions."

Often people think that they have a good argument for a conclusion because they have overlooked the fact that they have equivocated on one of their terms. For example, a Christian believer might argue that if we can believe in the miracle of putting a man on the moon, then we certainly can believe in the miracles of the Bible. The problem here is that the believer has overlooked his equivocation on the term "miracle." In its first occurrence it means wonderful achievement of human beings. In the second occurrence it means an event contrary to the laws of nature. These clearly are two different things. God performs miracles by suspending the laws of nature. Human beings, however, did not put a man on the moon by suspending the laws of nature--in fact they used the laws of nature to do it.

Fallacy of Composition

If we assume that what is true of a part must be true of the whole, we commit the fallacy of composition. This is often called the part-whole fallacy because it involves the comparison between parts and the wholes of which they are the parts. It is not necessarily true that what can be correctly said of a part can also be correctly said of the whole. For example, an art critic once said to a museum curator that the piece of modern art the museum had just acquired was ugly. The curator tried to defend his purchase by noting that the work was composed of crystals, each of which was very beautiful and, therefore,
the whole work must be beautiful. Saying this, of course, is like saying that since each brick in a building is light enough for a human being to pick up and carry that the whole building is too.

Fallacy of Division

Closely related to the fallacy of composition is the fallacy of division. This latter fallacy is the assumption that what is true of the whole or the group must be true of the parts of the whole or the members of the group. We would commit such an error if we were to conclude that we could not lift any one of the bricks in building because we cannot lift the whole building.

Both of these fallacies can occur in arguments that are formally valid. For example,

Birds are common to Canada and the kiwi is a bird. Therefore, the kiwi is common to Canada.

If you draw a Venn diagram for this argument, you will find that it is a valid categorical syllogism. But, in looking at the meaning of the terms and their arrangement in the argument, you will find that the informal fallacy of division has been committed. Consider another example:

Road-building was a typical activity of the ancient Romans. The construction of I-90 is road-building. Therefore, the construction of I-90 is a typical activity of the ancient Romans.

This, too, is a formally valid syllogism, but a poor argument because it commits the fallacy of division.

Exercise 27   Student: _____

Read the following arguments and determine what kind of fallacy has been committed. Give both the traditional name of the fallacy as well as an explanation of precisely where in the argument the mistake occurs and why it is a mistake.

1. Brother Infirmarian tells me that old Brother Matthew will soon die because his heart has become enlarged. This is no surprise to me, for we always knew that kind old Matthew was big-hearted.

    Fallacy name: _____

    Explanation: _____

    _____

    _____

2. Each part of Brother Albert is smaller than Brother Albert. It follows that all of Brother Albert is smaller than Brother Albert!

    Fallacy name: _____

    Explanation: _____

    _____

    _____

3. It says here in Aristotle's book that bees keep honey in combs and it says here in Thucydides' book that Solon the lawgiver kept a comb near his bed to use on his beard. The ancient authorities testify, then, that Solon used honey on his beard.

    Fallacy name: _____

    Explanation: _____

    _____

    _____

§18 Fallacies of Causation

Much of our reasoning is about cause and effect. We often use argument to prove that one thing is the cause of another. If, however, we make a mistake in our reasoning when trying to find a cause of something, then we commit a fallacy. Failure to avoid such a fallacy results in the mistaken assumption that we have found the cause for something when we really have not. There are many ways of making mistakes about causes. Two of the most common are described below.

False Cause

When two events happen close together in time and space, we might be tempted to say that one of them is the cause of the other. Temporal and spacial contiguousness, however, is usually not enough evidence to claim that one is the cause of the other. For example, a person at a meeting might start to cough at the same time that another person enters the room. Without more evidence, it is certainly jumping to a conclusion to say that the person's entering the room is the cause of the other person's cough. This kind of fallacy is often called by its Latin name: "post hoc, ergo propter hoc" which means "after this, therefore because of this." This kind of mistake can be seen in the following:

> The abbot stepped out into the garden just when the gardener, Brother Mark, sneezed. Clearly, Brother Mark is allergic to the abbot.

Here the arguer is drawing the conclusion that the cause of Brother Mark's sneeze is the presence of the abbot. If the only evidence for this conclusion is the observation of the sneeze taking place at the same time as the abbot comes near Brother Mark, the fallacy of false cause has been committed. The juxtaposition of the two events in time and place is not enough, by itself, to justify the conclusion that they are causally related.

Sometimes making this kind of mistake affects our actions. For example, in a famous battle, a military commander assumed that the withdrawal of the enemy's line was due the enemy's fear of his own approaching forces. In fact, the enemy's withdrawal was a tactical retreat which drew the commander's forces into an exposed position which cost him the battle. The commander's mistake was to assume the cause to be his army's approach and to overlook other possible causes for the enemy's withdrawal.

Common Cause

Another mistake we sometimes make about causes is the fallacy of common cause. This is the assumption that two events are related as cause and effect when in fact they are both effects of another event which is the cause of both. This fallacy is often committed when we do not understand the phenomena we are investigating very well or where we have a lack of information. For example, a field officer in the army might observe the enemy advancing on his left while his own forces are withdrawing. He might then draw the conclusion that these two events are causally related--either the enemy is forcing his army to withdraw on the left or the withdrawal on the left is drawing the enemy forward into the vacuum. But this conclusion might be due to limited intelligence. If the officer could see the whole picture, he might realize that both of these events are caused by the enemy's advance in the center--his own left withdrawing to keep pace with the withdrawing center and the enemy right advancing to support the advancing enemy center.

Common cause fallacies are often found in scientific reasoning where the scientist is faced with a little understood phenomenon. The early researcher of electricity, Michael Faraday, noticed that, under certain conditions, both a chemical action and electrical activity were produced. From this he concluded that the chemical action caused the electrical activity. He overlooked, however, the importance of the conditions in which both were present, namely that heat was always present beforehand and that heat causes both chemical action and electrical activity. Thus, his argument did not validly yield the conclusion that chemical action causes electrical activity.

Exercise 28   Student: _____

Read the following arguments and determine what kind of fallacy has been committed. Give both the traditional name of the fallacy as well as an explanation of precisely where in the argument the mistake occurs and why it is a mistake.

1.   I noticed that the cat came into the chapter room just as the abbot was rising to leave. Clearly, the abbot dislikes cats.

      Fallacy name: _____

      Explanation: _____

      _____

      _____

2.   Just as your novice brought in the wine, Reverand Abbot, I looked over at you and noticed you looking at me and that is when I began to cough. You must be wishing that I get ill.

      Fallacy name: _____

      Explanation: _____

      _____

      _____

3.   It can only be that the young novice working on the monastery accounts learned his accounting from Brother Stephen, because they both write their numbers in the same unusual way.

      Fallacy name: _____

      Explanation: _____

      _____

      _____

§19 Fallacies of Presumption

In all arguments which are formally valid, a relationship of necessity exists between the premises and the conclusion. Because, however, no conclusion can be more reliable than the premises on which they are based, it is important that our premises be well chosen and true. If we make a mistake in selecting our premises or in thinking them true when they are really false, we commit a fallacy of presumption. There are many ways in which our premises may turn out to be unreliable. Some of the most important are described below.

Hasty Generalization

In many of our arguments we are trying to prove that a universal proposition is true. If we attempt to draw such a conclusion from premises which really do not provide sufficient evidence for our generalization (universal conclusion), then we commit the fallacy of hasty generalization. This is the sort of conclusion that someone who was feeling sorry for himself might draw:

I will never learn geometry. Every time I try to understand a theorem, I get confused.

The man who is thinking like this is perhaps too hasty in concluding that he will never learn geometry. Just because he has not yet understood it does not means that is it impossible that he will ever come to understand it. Perhaps he has just not put forth enough effort yet.

When we speak of prejudice, we are often speaking of hasty generalizations. For example, a person who has just arrived in a new place might draw the conclusion that because every person he has met so far has been cold to him, that everybody there is cold. This is a fallacy because he does not have enough evidence yet to draw such a general conclusion. Ethic prejudice is often based on hasty generalizations. To conclude that all Frenchmen are arrogant on the basis of the three arrogant French waiters you met--who are the only Frenchmen you know--is fallacious. How do you know that the very next Frenchman you meet will not be very friendly?

Sweeping Generalization

Closely related to hasty generalization is the fallacy of sweeping generalization. Here one is not drawing a universal conclusion, but is drawing a conclusion from a universal premise in an improper way. This is the kind of mistake we make when we start from a general rule (our universal premise) and try to conclude to a specific case which we claim falls under the rule. If the specific case does not really fit the rule, then we commit the fallacy of sweeping generalization. Our general rule "sweeps in" too many cases. For example,

> Everyone has a right to his own property. Alexias, who is drunk and angry with Lysis, has just come to me to get back his sword which he lent me. I, therefore, must return it to him even though I know that he will, in his rage, kill Lysis with it.

It is true that anyone who lends something to somebody else has a right to get it back. But the case of a drunk and angry friend is an exceptional case and does not fall under the rule in the usual way. To assume that it does, as the arguer does here, is to be guilty of sweeping generalization. Another example is:

> It is always wrong to lie. Therefore, when the Gestapo agent asks me to tell him where my Jewish friends are hiding, I am under a moral obligation to tell him the truth.

Usually it is wrong to lie, but perhaps this is an unusual case and it would be morally better to lie.

Begging the Question

The primary purpose of argumentation is the advancement of our knowledge. In other words, we begin with what we already know (our premises) and conclude to what we do not yet know. This is the point of studying valid forms of argument. We want to be sure that our arguments are reliable in leading us to new knowledge. It is, however, possible that we might have a valid argument which does not lead us to new knowledge. To put this another way, we might start out assuming that a proposition is true and conclude that the same proposition is therefore true. Such an argument is formally valid (after all, from the standpoint of formal validity, the safest possible conclusion one can draw from a proposition is that proposition itself), but I have not really proved anything. I have only argued in a circle. The argument has not brought me any new knowledge. For example:

> Belief in God is universal, because everybody believes in a supreme divine being.

The argument here is valid, but it is just going around in a circle. To say that belief in God is universal is to say that everybody believes in a supreme divine being. In other words, these two clauses express the very same proposition in different words. Thus, this argument amounts to saying that everybody believes in God because everybody believes in God. That is not invalid but it is not very informative either. To argue in such a way that your conclusion is really one of your premises (perhaps stated in different words) is to beg the question. Begging the question like this is to argue in a circle and for this reason it is sometimes called "circular reasoning." When we beg the question we assume as true (in one of our premises) what we are trying to prove is true (in our conclusion). When we do this, of course, we have not really proven our conclusion is true, because its truth depends on our already accepting it as true. Another common example, which perhaps you have heard yourself, is the following:

God exists because the Bible says so and we know that what the Bible says is true because God inspired it.

The conclusion here, God exists, is based on three premises:

The Bible says that God exists.
Anything inspired by God must tell the truth.
The Bible is inspired by God.
God exists.

But these three premises have hidden in them a fourth premise, God exists, because the third premise implies it. In other words, for it to be true that God inspired the Bible, there must be a God. The only way we could know that it is true that God inspired the Bible is to already know that God exists. Thus, the argument is going around in a circle and the question which the argument sets out to answer "Does God exist?" goes begging to be proved, because this argument has not proved it is true, but simply assumed it is true.

False Analogy

An analogy is a comparison between two objects. Sometimes we use analogies in our arguments when we wish to prove something is true of an obscure or difficult to understand object by showing that the same thing is true of another object which is like it. If the two objects are enough alike, then we may have a good (even if not absolutely foolproof) argument in favor of our claim that something is true of the difficult to understand object. If, however, the two objects we are comparing are not enough alike or are not alike in the right sort of ways (though they may be alike in other ways), we may be guilty of false analogy. So, false analogy is a bad comparison used in an argument. For example, if someone argues that it is right to take money from other people because it's right for the government to take money from people in the form of taxes, he commits the fallacy of false analogy. The two cases are different in important ways which the arguer is ignoring here.

False Dichotomy

Often in our arguments we make use of a set of alternatives. Alternatives are expressed in disjunctive propositions such as "Either I will attend the meeting or my assistant will attend or my supervisor will attend." In this case there are three alternatives. We have already seen that if we can show that the same result occurs no matter which of the alternatives is true, then as long as at least one of them is true the result is true. This is the valid form of argument we call dilemma. Thus, say I know that no matter which of the alternatives given above is true, the result that our office will be represented at the meeting will be true. Say I also know that at least one of the alternatives is true, that is, at least one of us will attend. I can then conclude that it is true that our office will be represented at the meeting. This is a typical constructive dilemma.

The validity of this kind of argument, however, depends on the truth of the disjunction stating the alternatives. In other words, at least one of the alternatives must be true. Otherwise, the conclusion does not follow. But say that these alternatives are not exhaustive, that there are other possibilities. In this case all three of these alternatives might be false and my argument fails to prove the conclusion. Whenever we argue from a set of alternatives we must be sure that they represent all the possible alternatives that are relevant to what we are trying to prove. If we fail to do this, we commit the fallacy of false dichotomy. A false dichotomy is the presumption that a set of alternatives, a distinction, or a classification is exclusive and exhaustive when, in fact, other alternatives exist. Consider, for example, the following:

Either you are a Persian or you are not civilized.

This is a false dichotomy, because it claims that there are only two possibilities: being Persian (and civilized) and not being Persian (and therefore not civilized). In reality, however, there are other possibilities: I might be a civilized Greek or a civilized Chinese, etc.

It is important to note that not all dichotomies are false. If you have really covered all the possibilities, then you may have a true dichotomy. This is the case with "You are either dead or alive." There really don't seem to be other possibilities here. If true dichotomies were not possible, then there could never be a valid dilemma. If we can show that our set of alternatives is exhaustive, then we can use them in valid dilemmas.

Exercise 29   Student: _____

In Exercise 8, we encountered examples of universal propositions with subject terms referring to a particular individual. For example, "Socrates is wise" is a universal proposition with the subject term "Socrates" which refers to the particular person with that name. Other universal propositions have subject terms which refer to a group of things or a type of things. For example, "Egyptians are religious people" does not refer to a particular individual person, but to whole group of people. These two different kinds of universal propositions can be distinguished:

Universal Particularization: This is a universal proposition with a subject term which refers to a particular individual person or thing. In a universal particularization, the subject term is often a name or definite description which picks out a particular individual. The following are all examples of universal particularization:

[1] Alcuin was a great biblical scholar.

[2] The castle at Pavia is impregnable.

[3] The book on the lectern was written by Alcuin.

Universal Generalization: This is a universal proposition with a subject term which refers to a group of individual persons or things or to a kind of thing. In a universal generalization, the subject term will be the name or description of a group or the name of a kind of thing. The following are all examples of universal generalization:

[4] The Franks were brave warriors.

[5] All of the emperor's soldiers are well-trained.

[6] Every animal possesses tactile organs.

The fallacies of hasty generalization and sweeping generalization are mistakes we make when using universal generalizations in arguments. When we hastily generalize, we conclude to a universal generalization in an inductive argument without sufficient evidence in our premises. When we commit the fallacy of sweeping generalization, we misapply the universal generalization in our premises to a particular case in our conclusion.

In order to accurately analyze cases of these fallacies, it is important that we are able to distinguish clearly between the two kinds of universal propositions. For each of the following universal propositions, write out the subject term and indicate whether the proposition is a universal praticular or a universal generalization.

1.	Armenian Christians are very pious people.

_____

universal particular/universal generalization

2.	The Armenian Patriarch is a very pious man.

_____

universal particular/universal generalization

3.	Armenian Christians serving in the Roman army refused to worship the pagan gods.

_____

universal particular/universal generalization

4.	All Christians living in Armenia worship in the Armenian language.

_____

universal particular/universal generalization

5.	John of Nicaea translated Aristotle's treatise on physics from Greek into Armenian.

_____

universal particular/universal generalization

6.	All of Aristotle's books have been translated into the Armenian language.

_____

universal particular/universal generalization

Exercise 30   Student: _____

Read the following arguments and determine what kind of fallacy has been committed. Give both the traditional name of the fallacy as well as an explanation of precisely where in the argument the mistake occurs and why it is a mistake.

1.   Sir Morgan is clearly guilty of cowardice, because he is a man afraid to face danger. That is all I need to know to know that he is guilty.

      Fallacy name: _____

      Explanation: _____

      _____

      _____

2.   Just as an eaglet who strays from the nest too soon will certainly die, Reverand Abbot, my son who has left his native city on his fourteenth birthday will never come back again alive.

      Fallacy name: _____

      Explanation: _____

      _____

      _____

3.   Aristotle argued that deer have horns for the sake of defense and that defense is a benefit to them. This is certainly correct, for deer benefit from horns.

      Fallacy name: _____

      Explanation: _____

      _____

      _____

4.   All Turks are weak. I saw one yesterday in the infirmary and he was so weak he could not stand.

Fallacy name: _____

Explanation: _____

_____

_____

5.   Prince William has only two choices, to remain in the city as a supporter of his father or to leave the city in rejection of his father's claim to the throne. In either case he will be a coward.

Fallacy name: _____

Explanation: _____

_____

_____

6.   All Normans are tall. Therefore, this Norman infant is tall.

Fallacy name: _____

Explanation: _____

_____

_____

§20 Fallacies of Relevance

In a good argument it should be clear that the premises are related in content to the conclusion. The conclusion, after all, is made necessarily true by the premises, assuming that the premises are true. Sometimes, however, it may seem that our premises are relevant to our conclusion when, in fact, they really are not. There are many types of fallacies of relevance and some of the more important are described below.

Argumentum ad misericordiam

One of the most common kinds of fallacies of relevance is the appeal to pity or other emotion. This is a very old fallacy and is still often known by its ancient Latin name "argumentum ad misericordiam" which means argument from pity. We commit this fallacy when we try to win approval of our conclusion by playing on the emotions of others. This is the kind of argument recommended by the ancient Roman professor who told his students that he could show them how to win over any jury if they are brought to court, no matter how bad their case really is. All you have to do, he suggested, is to dress your wife and children in rags and bring them into court. Make sure that you bring in your youngest children and if you don't have any then borrow some from a neighbor. And make sure they are all crying. And if they are not, rub their eyes with onion so that they will shed many tears. Seeing your poverty-stricken family like this, the jury will feel sorry for you and, even if you are guilty of the worst crime, will acquit you out of pity. Of course, whether your family is poor or not or whether your children are happy or not is irrelevant to the question of whether you are guilty. The Roman professor is urging his students to commit the fallacy of argumentum ad misericordiam.

Argumentum ad ignorantiam

Usually when we are trying to prove a conclusion we try to show what the evidence in its favor is and present this evidence in our premises. If, on the other hand, we argue that, because there is no evidence against the conclusion, it must be true, we commit the fallacy of arguing from ignorance. The person who claims that a conclusion is true has the burden of proving it by giving evidence that it is true--that is, by showing that some true premises logically lead to the conclusion. To say that we don't know that something is not true does not prove that it is true. For example, one often hears this kind of argument:

No one has proven that there are not intelligent beings living on other planets. Therefore, there are such beings on other planets.

Just because no one has proven otherwise does not prove that something must be true. The burden of proof here is on the person who makes the claim that intelligent beings exist on other planets. If he wants to argue that this is true, he must present the evidence that it is true--that is, he must find true premises which necessitate the conclusion that such beings exist on other planets.

Argumentum ad hominem

Probably the most common fallacy of relevance is attacking the person making an argument in an effort to show that the argument is invalid. Such attacking the arguer instead of his argument is called argumentum ad hominem (argument against the person). These kinds of attacks can be made in several different ways. Some of the most common are described below.

Abusive ad hominem

The way in which a reasonable person would attack the truth of a conclusion is to show that the arguer's premises do not really lead to the conclusion (that the argument for the conclusion is invalid) or that the premises, even if they do lead to the conclusion, are not true. Sometimes, however, we try to show that a conclusion is false by attacking the character of the person drawing the conclusion. The arguer's character, of course, is irrelevant to the validity of his argument or to the truth of his premises. When we attack the arguer instead of his argument in this way, we commit the fallacy of abusive ad hominem. For example, this argument attacks the character of a judge instead of the reasons for his decision:

> The judge's decision is obviously invalid and should be appealed. This judge, after all, is known to be corrupt and only holds his office because he is a relative of the Chief Justice.

Whether the judge's decision is right or wrong is a matter of the law and arguments based on the law. Even if it is true that he is corrupt, his decision might still be right. The only rational way to show that his decision is wrong is to show that his argument leading to the decision is invalid or that his premises are false.

Circumstantial ad hominem

Another kind of ad hominem fallacy occurs when we claim that someone's conclusion must be false because that person has a personal interest in its being true or because of some other circumstances. If we argue against someone in this way instead of trying to show that his argument is invalid or his premises false, then we commit a circumstantial ad hominem fallacy. For example:

Dr. Nakkanishi has argued that his new drug will be effective. But we do not have to take his argument seriously because he clearly stands to make a lot of money if the drug is approved.

Even if it is true that Dr. Nakkanishi will become rich if the drug is approved, that alone does not prove that his argument--based, say, on clinical trials--is not effective. If you want to show that his drug is not effective you have to show that his evidence is insufficient, not what will happen to his bank account upon approval.

Tu quoque

Another kind of ad hominem fallacy is the sort we commit when we try to show that someone's conclusion is false by saying "look who's talking." In other words, instead of showing that there are logical or factual mistakes in another's argument, we try to reject the argument on the grounds that the arguer does not follow his own advice or accept his own conclusion. For example:

Both of my parents have been urging me with lots of arguments about my health to give up smoking. But I don't take their arguments very seriously because both of my parents have always been heavy smokers. If they really want to prove to me that they are right, they should stop smoking themselves.

Here the arguer is claiming that his parents' conclusion about the bad effects of smoking on health is false on the grounds that his parents are smokers--that is, that they are not taking their own advice. Of course, this does not prove that his parents' arguments are invalid and smoking really is not unhealthful. At best it shows that his parents find giving up smoking as difficult as he does. If the arguer wants to show that his parents' arguments are invalid, he must attack the arguments, not his parents' actions.

Another version of the tu quoque fallacy is the "they do it too" argument. If someone argues that it is permissible for our country to commit illegal acts in other countries because other countries do the same thing, one commits this fallacy. There may be good reasons to commit illegal acts in other countries, but it cannot be simply that other countries do it too.

Exercise 31   Student: _____

Read the following arguments and determine what kind of fallacy has been committed. Give both the traditional name of the fallacy as well as an explanation of precisely where in the argument the mistake occurs and why it is a mistake.

1.   We have lost contact with the Norman cavalry and we do not know where they are now. You cannot prove that they are not about to attack our right flank. Therefore, it is impossible that they will fail to attack us on the right.

      Fallacy name: _____

      Explanation: _____

      _____

      _____

2.   Reverand Father, you are a priest and so you live without a wife. Therefore, you are in no position to argue that wife-beating is evil.

      Fallacy name: _____

      Explanation: _____

      _____

      _____

3.   The Greek Patriarch argued that it was a sin against God and man to attack innocent people. But he did not say this when the Greeks attacked the innocent town. Therefore, it must be permissible in God's eyes to attack the innocent.

      Fallacy name: _____

      Explanation: _____

      _____

      _____

4.	Yes, it is true that those knights robbed the villagers of their livestock. But you must understand that they were unjustly treated by the king and so their act was justified.

Fallacy name: _____

Explanation: _____

_____

_____

Appendix I: Pseudo-Socratic Dialogues

The ancient Greek philosopher Plato (427-348BC) wrote many dialogues in which his teacher, Socrates (469-399BC), was one of the speakers. These dialogues present us with philosophical conversations between Socrates and his friends. The dialogues in this appendix are not by Plato, but they are inspired by his work. None of them is historical, though some of the characters in them really existed. They are all set in the ancient Greek city-state of Athens, where Socrates taught and where his most famous student, Plato, later established his school known as the Academy.

Use these dialogues as additional exercises. They will provide you with practice recognizing and evaluating the types of arguments you have studied in this book. For each dialogue, read it carefully and then answer the questions which follow.

Student: _____

The Remarks of Zeno

Walking home one day Socrates noticed a veiled young woman standing thoughtfully near the tomb of Academos. As he came closer he realized that it was Axiothea of Phlius, the daughter of an old friend of his. As he approached, he greeted her and asked:

Socrates: Why do you linger here, Axiothea, will they not be missing you at home?

Axiothea: No, Socrates, they know at home that I came here to see you. I did not want to disturb you at your reading and I decided to wait for you here, knowing that you would pass by.

Socrates: Why are you so anxious to see me?

Axiothea: It is because I heard Zeno the Sophist speaking in the Market Place yesterday. I have been thinking of his words ever since and I wish to ask you about them.

Socrates: Of what did Zeno speak?

Axiothea: Of many things, Socrates. Among them was the claim that no woman can be a philosopher. He asserted that this claim is true. Yet only last month you told my friend Lasthenia that she had made such progress in her studies that she can justly be considered a true philosopher.

Socrates: Yes, Lasthenia does indeed have the soul of the true philosopher.

Axiothea: If what you say is true, then Zeno's claim cannot also be true.

Socrates: Your reasoning is flawless, Axiothea. Did Zeno make any other claims?

Axiothea: Yes, he also claimed that saying that all philosophers are men is the same as saying that all men are philosophers. But this cannot be correct, can it Socrates?

Socrates: Let us investigate the matter and see. Tell me, are Zeno's two propositions affirmative or negative?

Axiothea: They are clearly affirmative.

Socrates: Do they apply to all the cases they speak of or only some.

Axiothea: They are universal.

Socrates:	Good. Now, do the two propositions share the same terms or do they differ in their terms?
Axiothea:	They share the same terms. One term is being human and the other is being a philosopher.
Socrates:	Thus, the two propositions are the same in many ways.
Axiothea:	They are indeed the same in many ways, but they differ in one respect: the second is the converse of the first. Is this why they seem to say different things?
Socrates:	If this is the only way in which they differ and they truly say different things, this difference must be the reason why they have different meanings.
Axiothea:	It certainly is true that all philosophers are human beings. But it does not seem true to say that all human beings are philosophers. Now, if I understand you, Socrates, you are suggesting that the reason why these two propositions are different in meaning is because one is the converse of the other.
Socrates:	Yes, that is correct. Please hand me that stick over there. Now, I will draw a diagram for each of these propositions in the dust of the road here.
Axiothea:	[looking at Socrates' diagrams] I see clearly now that Zeno's two propositions cannot mean the same thing.

1.   Why does Axiothea think that Zeno's claim about women being philosophers cannot be true if Socrates' claim that Lasthenia (who is a woman) is a philosopher is true?

_____

_____

2.   Assuming that Socrates drew Venn diagrams in the road, what would his diagrams have looked like?

3.   What do Socrates' diagrams show about Zeno's two propositions?

_____

_____

4.   What does Axiothea mean when she says that Zeno's two propositions cannot mean the same thing?

_____

_____

_____

On the Triangle

Socrates and his friend Cebes are standing outside a wine shop near the Market Place discussing a mathematical problem.

Cebes: Look, Socrates, here comes that young man Satyros. I don't know why you tolerate him in your presence. He is arrogant and has the logical skills of a pomegranate.

Socrates: Now Cebes, you must be kind. Remember that patience is a virtue. Besides, it is the task of philosophy to raise the mind from ignorance to knowledge. Perhaps, we owe it to philosophy to help train the young to good habits of reasoning.

Cebes: I will tolerate him for the sake of philosophy.

Satyros: Greetings Socrates! Greetings Cebes! I see from your drawing in the sand that you are doing some geometry.

Cebes: That is correct, Satyros. Perhaps you would care to join us.

Satyros: I would. I have a special aptitude for geometry. I first became aware of my great talent for this subject when Nicostratus praised my drawings of hexagons. As Nicostratus is over two hundred years old, we can be sure that his praise of me is based on his wisdom.

Cebes: Two hundred years old! Where did you hear that, Satyros?

Satyros: I did not hear it anywhere. I figured it out for myself.

Socrates: Please enlighten us on your remarkable method of deducing the age of such a venerable man.

Satyros: It is easy, Socrates. As you know, Nicostratus is a member of the Pythagorean brotherhood. That brotherhood is over two hundred years old. Clearly it follows that Nicostratus is at least two hundred years old.

Cebes: What nonsense! That is the most obvious fallacy I ever . . .

Socrates: [laying his hand on Cebes' sleeve] I am certain, Cebes, that Satyros will carefully examine what he has just told us and discover his fallacy for himself. Might we return to the discussion we were having when our young friend joined us?

Satyros:	Yes, of course, gentlemen. Please continue your mathematical discourse.
Socrates:	Now, if we will return our attention to the diagram we have drawn here and intersect this line here with another line at this point, we will find that we have an obtuse triangle.
Satyros:	Indeed you have and that gives us an ignorant triangle.
Cebes:	An ignorant triangle! What is an ignorant triangle?
Satyros:	This is. It follows by a clear syllogism: some triangles are obtuse, are they not?
Cebes:	Yes.
Satyros:	Whatever is obtuse is ignorant. Therefore, some triangles are ignorant. This is one.
Cebes:	But . . .
Socrates:	[again, laying his hand on Cebes' sleeve] I am certain that Satyros is aware of his error and is only testing our wit. Let us continue. In a figure such as this, one can measure the length of this line between the points at which these two lines intersect.
Satyros:	Excuse me, Socrates, but I am afraid I must correct you. Lines cannot have length.
Socrates:	Why not, Satyros?
Satyros:	Every line is composed of points. This is true, is it not?
Socrates:	Yes it is, Satyros.
Satyros:	No point has length. This is also true, is it not?
Socrates:	Yes, points lack both length and breadth.
Satyros:	The conclusion is obvious: lines lack length.
Socrates:	Satyros, can you detect an error in your reasoning?
Satyros:	Certainly not, Socrates. My argument is valid. If lines lack length, then they are made out of points. We all agree that lines are composed of points. Therefore, lines lack length.

Cebes: [walking away] I leave you the joy of the education of this young man, Socrates!

Satyros: What did I say?

1.   What is the fallacy that Satyros commits when he explains how he figured out the age of Nicostratus? (Give the traditional name of the fallacy and explain exactly where it occurs in his explanation.)

      Fallacy name: _____

      Explanation: _____

      _____

      _____

2.   What is the logical form of Satyros' argument that some triangles are ignorant? (Give a schematic representation of the argument using any term letters you wish.)

3.   Is Satyros' argument valid?   Yes __ No __

4.   If you answered "yes" to 3, then draw a Venn diagram for Satyros' argument. If you answered "no" to 3, then skip to the next question.

5.   Explain why Satyros' argument about ignorant triangles is invalid.

6. What is Satyros' first argument that lines cannot have length? (Give a schematic representation of the argument using any term letters you wish.)

7. Is this argument of Satyros valid? Yes __ No __

8. If you answered "yes" to 7, draw a Venn diagram of the argument. If you answered "no" to 7, skip to the next question.

9. Why is Satyros' argument invalid?

_____

_____

_____

10. What is the logical form of Satyros' second argument that lines lack length? (Give a schematic representation of the argument using any schematic letters you wish.)

11. What is the traditional name for this kind of argument?

_____

12. Is this argument valid? Yes __ No __

Dialogue 3   Student: _____

On Alcibiades (I)

Two citizens of ancient Athens were walking together near the temple of Athena discussing a famous student of Socrates.

Philon: If Alcibiades is unjust, it is absurd to blame his teacher Socrates for it.

Myron: A teacher has to answer for his pupil.

Philon: I have not seen Alcibiades with Socrates for many years.

Myron: Even so, Socrates claimed to make his pupils better. If Alcibiades left Socrates for good reason, then Socrates gave him cause and is to blame. If he left Socrates for no good reason, then Socrates did not teach him justice and is still to blame. No matter which, Socrates is answerable for the injustice in his former pupil.

1.   What is the logical form of Myron's argument that Socrates is to blame for Alcibiades' injustice? (Give a schematic representation of the argument using any schematic letters you wish.)

2.   What is the traditional name for this sort of argument?

       _____

3.   Is the argument valid?   Yes __   No __

Dialogue 4   Student: _____

On Alcibiades (II)

Two citizens of ancient Athens were walking together near the Market Place discussing a famous student of Socrates.

Myron: They say in the streets that Alcibiades is to blame for the sacrilege and I can believe it.

Philon: You were always ready to believe the worst of him, but this time you are wrong. After all he was Socrates' pupil.

Myron: All the more reason. We know that Socrates refused to be initiated into the holy mysteries. If this is true, then Socrates has no respect for religious custom. If he lacks respect for sacred custom, then he is guilty of sacrilege. Thus, his refusal to be initiated clearly implies his guilt.

Philon: I do not accept your premises, but even if you are correct what has this to do with Alcibiades?

Myron: Only this sir: if a teacher is guilty of sacrilege, as we know Socrates is, such is what he teaches his pupils.

1.   What is the logical form of Myron's argument that Socrates' refusal to be initiated into the mysteries shows he is guilty of sacrilege? (Give a schematic representation of the argument using any schematic letters you wish.)

2.   What is the traditional name for this kind of argument?

      _____

3.   Is this argument valid? Yes __ No __

4. Philon says that he does not accept Myron's premises. What does he mean by this?

_____

_____

_____

5. Is it possible that Philon consider Myron's argument valid even though he does not accept Myron's premises? Why or why not?

_____

_____

_____

6. Why does Myron believe that Socrates teaches his students sacrilege? (Write out the premises of Myron's argument.)

_____

_____

_____

_____

7. What kind of argument is Myron using here? (Give the traditional name of the argument form.)

_____

On Pleasure

Walking through the Market Place one day, Socrates joins a discussion between his friend Lysis and Nichoros of Sardis, just as Lysis is leaving.

Socrates: Greetings Nichoros! I overheard your discussion with Lysis just now and I am interested in how you would defend your view that pleasure is the highest good.

Nichoros: As you saw, Lysis had to leave before I finished my argument and I will be very pleased to take the matter up with you.

Socrates: Very good! Now, you wish to claim that pleasure--by which I assume you mean bodily pleasures such as eating, drinking, sexual pleasures, and the like--is the highest good. Most people, if asked what is the highest good would say that it is happiness. Would you disagree?

Nichoros: No, not at all.

Socrates: I see. So you would argue that given that happiness is what we call the highest good and the highest good is pleasure, then we can conclude that what we call happiness is pleasure.

Nichoros: That is exactly what I argue.

Socrates: This amounts to saying that happiness is identical with pleasure. Do you agree?

Nichoros: Yes.

Socrates: If this is the case, then we are happy only when we are experiencing physical pleasures. But this is not the only time when we are happy. Cannot an athlete, for example, be in pain due to his training, but still be happy? It seems that we must conclude that happiness is not identical with pleasure.

Nichoros: I agree with you when you say that if happiness is identical with pleasure, then we are happy when we have pleasure. But who would deny we are happy when we are experiencing pleasure? No one, I submit. Therefore, happiness is identical with pleasure.

Socrates: A close look at your argument will convince you that you have made a serious error. But let us go on with the matter at hand. Do you agree that any pleasure is capable of being lost?

Nichoros: I do.

Socrates: Is it not also true that anything which can be lost cannot really bring happiness?

Nichoros: Yes.

Socrates: Must we not conclude that nothing that is pleasure can be true happiness?

Nichoros: I suppose we must. But we still consider pleasure that which makes us feel good. Do we not also feel good when we are happy?

Socrates: Nichoros, you must be careful of making false analogies!

Nichoros: What about this, Socrates? When I get up in the morning and feel good--well rested, free of pain, and so on--I often say "Oh, I am happy today!" or "What a happy day!" I certainly mean the same when, in thinking about my life as a whole, I say "I am a happy man!" or "What a happy life I lead!"

Socrates: Another fallacy! Give me your tablets. I am going to write down the name of a good logician I know who can cure you of your poor habits of reasoning. I recommend that you see him.

1. Toward the beginning of the dialogue, Socrates reconstructs Nichoros' argument that happiness is identical to pleasure. What are the premises of this argument?

   Premise 1: _____

   _____

   Premise 2: _____

   _____

2. What is the logical form of this argument? (Give a schematic representation of the argument.)

3.   What is the traditional name for this sort of argument?

        _____

4.   Is the argument valid?   Yes___   No___   Prove it.

5.   Socrates gives an argument against the claim that happiness is identical with pleasure. Can
        his argument be reconstructed as a reductio ad absurdum argument? If it can write out the
        premise assumed for the sake of argument, the contradiction, and the conclusion. If it
        cannot, explain why?

        _____

        _____

        _____

        _____

        _____

        _____

6.   Nichoros counter-attacks with another argument. What is the logical form of his
        argument? (Give a schematic representation of the argument using any schematic letters
        you wish.)

7. Socrates claims that Nichoros has argued fallaciously.

Is Socrates correct? Yes__ No__

If you answered "yes," then explain where Nichoros makes his mistake. If you answered "no," then explain why Nichoros' argument is valid.

_____

_____

_____

_____

8. What is the logical form of Socrates' argument showing that pleasure cannot be happiness because it can be lost? (Give a schematic representation of the argument using any schematic letters you wish.)

9. Can you prove that Socrates' argument is valid? If so, prove it.

10. What is the false analogy which Socrates accuses Nichoros of making?

_____

_____

_____

11. What is the final fallacy which Nichoros commits and which part of the argument does it concern?

_____

_____

_____

On Good Decisions

Socrates had been invited to dinner at the home of Lysis. After a fine meal of tunny in aspic, the wine came around. Lysis' old father, however, excused himself and, saying "good night" to his guest, he retired. Left to themselves, Lysis and Socrates soon came around to the talk they had earlier that day in the Market Place.

Lysis: Myron made a foolish claim in the Assembly this morning. He said that the fact that the Assembly has made some good decisions shows that all of the Assembly's decisions are good.

Socrates: A foolish argument indeed!

Lysis: But is it not true that the record of the Assembly provides evidence that its future decisions will be sound--that is, assuming that the record is a good one?

Socrates: Yes, Lysis, but past good deeds do not assure that future deeds will be good. Arguing from the evidence in this sort of way provides relatively weak arguments. The only sort of argument which will assure that one is correct about the goodness of an act of the Assembly, past, present, or future, is one which has as its premise a universal.

Lysis: You mean that had Myron argued that because all of the Assembly's decisions are good therefore the Assembly has made some good decisions, he would have provided a valid inference.

Socrates: Yes, this is what I mean. With such an argument Myron would have provided an absolutely certain argument.

1.   What is the argument Myron actually makes before the Assembly? (Write out the premise and the conclusion.)

Premise: _____

_____

Conclusion: _____

_____

2.   Why does Socrates call it a foolish argument?

_____

_____

3.   What kind of argument is Lysis using when he says that the good record of the Assembly provides evidence that its future decisions will be good?

_____

4.   Why does Socrates say that this is a relatively weak form of argument? Relative to what?

_____

_____

_____

_____

_____

5.   What is the logical form of the argument Lysis thinks Myron should have given? (Give a schematic representation of the argument using any schematic letters you wish.)

Student: _____

The Soul of a Philosopher

Having spent most of the day in the Market Place, Socrates is just preparing to return home when he sees Axiothea and her mother coming toward him.

Socrates: [bowing to Axiothea's mother] Good day, madam. Greetings, Axiothea. I hope that this day finds both of you in good health.

Axiothea: We are well, Socrates. We have come looking for my father. Lysis told me that I might find him here.

Socrates: I have not seen him and I have been here all day. I understand that he was at the court of justice earlier today. Perhaps he has not yet finished his business there and will be here shortly.

Axiothea: While we wait, would you answer a question for me?

Socrates: Certainly.

Axiothea: Yesterday I accompanied my brother to the grove of Academos where we met Kritias. We fell into conversation and the question of whether women can have the souls of philosophers came up.

Socrates: I expect that you must have defended the affirmative, being both a woman and one dedicated to philosophy.

Axiothea: Indeed I did. But Kritias claimed that no woman is truly rational on the grounds that man is the only rational creature and no man is a woman. I agreed that his syllogism appeared valid, but I claimed that I was not rationally compelled to accept his conclusion.

Socrates: Was it because of the fallacy he commits in this argument?

Axiothea: Yes. I pointed it out to him, but I do not think that he understood. What can I say to him so that he comes to see his error?

Socrates: You must point out to him that one cannot both argue as he does and be rational. As he has in fact argued in this way, it clearly follows that he is not being rational.

1.	What is Kritias' argument? (Write out the premises and conclusion.)

	Premise 1: _____

	_____

	Premise 2: _____

	_____

	Conclusion: _____

	_____

2.	What is the fallacy which Axiothea and Socrates agree Kritias has committed? (Give both the traditional name of the fallacy and an explanation of where in the argument it occurs and how it makes the argument invalid.)

	Fallacy name: _____

	Explanation: _____

	_____

	_____

3.	If Kritias has committed a fallacy, why does Axiothea say that his argument appears valid? Does she mean that it really is valid?

	_____

	_____

	_____

	_____

	_____

	_____

4. What is the logical form of Socrates' argument that Kritias is not being rational? (Give a schematic representation of the argument using any schematic letters you wish.)

5. What is the traditional name for Socrates' argument?

_____

On the Fee of Protagoras

Sitting in his favorite wine shop with some friends, Socrates told a story about a famous teacher named Protagoras. This teacher, Socrates explained, did such a good job of teaching logic to his student Euathlus, that the skills Protagoras imparted were eventually used against him.

Protagoras: My dear Euathlus, you have studied with me for a whole year and I have imparted to you the skills which will make you a persuasive speaker before any court. Further, in my consideration for your poverty, I have agreed to put off collecting my teaching fee from you until you have won your first case. Do you agree that this is our arrangement?

Euathlus: Indeed I do, Protagoras.

Protagoras: Why, then, have you attempted to avoid paying me by refraining from all litigation?

Euathlus: Well, must I go to court, Protagoras?

Protagoras: You must if I sue you and then, no matter what happens, you will be forced to pay me my fee.

Euathlus: How can you be so sure?

Protagoras: It follows logically, young man, for consider that I am suing you for my fee-- indeed, I have just come from the law court where I have filed my petition with the clerks. Now, if you successfully defend yourself from my prosecution of this suit, then you win your first case and you must pay me my teaching fee according to our agreement. If, on the other hand, you are not successful and you lose the case, then you must pay me what I am suing you for, which is my teaching fee. Clearly, you must either win or lose the case. But no matter which happens, you must pay me.

Euathlus: It seems, Protagoras, that you are quite sure that I will be paying your fee.

Protagoras: I see no other outcome of this affair. It is simply a matter of logic.

Euathlus: And the reason that you seem so sure is that you think that you have me hung up on the horns of your dilemma, is that not correct?

Protagoras: How can it be otherwise?

Euathlus: Well, I might try to escape between the horns of your dilemma by denying that your disjunctive premise is true. After all, the judge might not make a decision--he might refuse to decide or disqualify himself from deciding or consider that the case is, on the evidence, undecidable.

Protagoras: Well . . . yes.

Euathlus: On the other hand, I might admit that your disjunction is true, but deny one of your conditional premises. Even if I won the case it does not follow that I will have to pay, because this is not the sort of case our original agreement was meant to cover.

Protagoras: But . . .

Euathlus: However, Protagoras, I will not argue in either of these ways. Instead, I will rebut your dilemma.

Protagoras: Impossible!

Euathlus: It is not impossible, if I can show that the same facts lead to the opposite conclusion.

Protagoras: How can you do that?

Euathlus: Consider the following argument. If I win the law suit which you are bringing against me, then I do not have to pay your fee by the judge's decision. If I lose, I do not have to pay by our agreement. No matter which happens, then, I do not have to pay your teaching fee.

Protagoras: [walking away muttering to himself] I am going to have to get out of the teaching business--I am too good at it!

1. What is the traditional name for the kind of argument Protagoras uses to prove that Euathlus must pay him?

2.	What are the premises of Protagoras' argument?

Premises: _____

_____

_____

_____

3.	What is the logical form of Protagoras' argument? (Give a schematic representation of his argument.)

4.	When Euathlus refers to the "horns" of Protagoras' dilemma, what is he talking about?

_____

5.	When Euathlus says that he might escape between the horns of Protagoras' dilemma, he is, in effect, accusing Protagoras of committing a fallacy. What is the fallacy and why is it a mistake?

Fallacy name: _____

Explanation: _____

_____

_____

_____

6.	Why does Euathlus think that denying one of Protagoras' conditional premises will defeat his teacher's argument?

7.	What is Euathlus' argument that he does not have to pay Protagoras' teaching fee? (Write out the premises and the conclusion.)

Premises: _____

_____

_____

_____

_____

_____

Conclusion: _____

_____

8.	What is the logical form of Euathlus' argument? (Give a schematic representation of his argument.)

Appendix II: Judge Dee Stories

Judge Dee Jen-djieh (630-700) lived during the Tang dynasty. Like most ancient Chinese magistrates, he was the chief law enforcement officer in the district in which he served and therefore, often engaged in detective work to solve crimes. While Judge Dee was a real person, the stories in this appendix are not historical. Nonetheless, they have something of the flavor of the many legends told about him in Chinese literature.

Use these stories as additional exercises. They will provide you with practice recognizing and evaluating the types of arguments you have studied in this book. For each story, read it carefully and then answer the questions which follow.

Judge Dee and the Case of the Paper Cat

The judge said to Sergeant Hoong, "I am afraid that our loyal assistant Lieutenant Chiao has made another error in reasoning. The murder of the five victims is not somehow the result of the presence of the folded paper cats just because the victims died shortly after receiving them."

"Does this mean that there is no connection at all?" asked the sergeant.

"Let us assume that there is a connection," began the judge. "If this were true, then there would have to be something different about the five paper cats that were sent to the murder victims that distinguished them from the twelve other paper cats sent to others who suffered no ill effects. But Dr. Kuo's examination showed absolutely no difference between the paper cats sent to the victims and those sent to others. We can only conclude that there is no connection."

The sergeant reflected that, once again, the judge, in his wisdom, was not led astray by poor reasoning.

1.   What is the fallacy committed by Lieutenant Chiao? (Give both the traditional name for the fallacy and explain why it is a logical error.)

Fallacy name: _____

Explanation: _____

_____

_____

2.   What is the logical form of the judge's argument? (Give a schematic representation of the argument.)

3.   What kind of argument is it? (Give the traditional name of the argument.)

_____

4.   Is the judge's argument valid?   Yes ___   No ___

Judge Dee Visits a Learned Abbot

The judge dismounted before the gate of the monastery. An elderly monk came out to meet him. Bowing low, the monk said, "I am the humble porter of this holy place and on behalf of our blessed Abbot Yu I welcome you." And handing the reins of the judge's horse to a novice, he led the judge to the abbot's study. After the judge had been welcomed with the usual formal courtesies and offered a cup of hot tea, the abbot said:

"You are here on a matter of parricide, are you not?"

"Yes," replied the judge.

"The foulest of crimes--to kill one's own father!"

"Indeed, Your Holiness!" remarked the judge. "I have come to see you because I want you to make a public statement on the seriousness of this crime and why the state is justified in its treatment of the guilty party. It seems that the citizens have turned against the tribunal because of their sympathy for the victim's son."

"I beg to be excused from this task, Your Honor. For I can only say that evil is a matter of the heart. No act is evil in itself."

"But surely," objected the judge, "you consider the murder of one's own parent a deed evil in itself?" Abbot Yu answered:

"A parricide is in the same relation to his father as a young oak to the parent tree, which, springing up from an acorn dropped by the parent, grows up and overturns it. We may search as we like, but we shall find no vice in this event. Therefore, there can be none in the other where the relation is just the same."

At this the judge took his leave and, riding back to the tribunal, reflected that Abbot Yu, for all his learning, was not beyond those errors of reasoning which are the blemish on the fruit of wisdom.

1.   What is the traditional name for the abbot's logical mistake?

_____

2.   Explain why the abbot's argument is fallacious.

_____

_____

_____

Judge Dee and the Boat Mystery

Judge Dee's usual stern expression suddenly changed to a self-satisfied look. He and his assistant Sergeant Hoong were standing on the tow path of the Grand Canal looking out at the shipping making its way toward the sea. The sergeant noticed the change which came over the judge's face and asked "What is it, Your Honor?" Still smiling the judge replied "Give an order for the arrest of Kuo Ming!"

Surprised, the sergeant forgot the rules of courtesy and blurted out "But how do you know that he is the smuggler?" The judge, overlooking the sergeant's unusual lapse of decorum, explained his reasoning. "Now sergeant, you will recall that all of the smuggled silk was packed in bright yellow boxes of an unusual sort. Anything packed in such boxes would be stained with that color. So, we can expect to find all of the silk stained in this way. Given that all the silk was stained like this and that anything stained yellow would be visible from far away, it is easy to see that all the silk would be visible from a distance. Now, anything visible from that distance would be visible from shore and so the silk should be visible from shore. If you would look at that second junk from the left, sergeant, you will see that the mystery is solved."

Looking at the boat indicated by the judge, the sergeant saw that the decks were covered with bolts of silk streaked with bright yellow. Then he too started to smile when he realized he was looking at Kuo Ming's junk.

1.   The judge pesents a complex argument demonstrating that Kuo Ming is guilty. How many parts does his argument contain?

        _____

2.   What is the logical form of his argument? (Give a schematic representation of the argument.)

3.   Is the judge's complex argument valid? Demonstrate that it is or is not.

Judge Dee and the Case of the Murdered Merchant

Although he was greatly disturbed by the puzzling case of the murder of the silk merchant Loo Ming, the judge told the assistant scribe to allow his caller to come in. He was very pleased to see that his visitor was Miss Tao, the daughter of his old friend the prefect Tao Kang. The judge once worked with the prefect when both were living in the Capital City and were members of an imperial commission. He had come to greatly respect the prefect's learning and dedication to public service. He remembered that Prefect Tao educated his daughter in the classics and that the young woman was a poetess of some renown. A stimulating conversation with someone of learning was just what he needed to take his mind off the troublesome case.

"I am very happy to see you, Miss Tao," said the judge. The young woman bowed respectfully to the judge and greeted him, passing on her father's greetings as well. After some small talk, Miss Tao said:

"My father told me how troubled you are over the death of the merchant Loo. If it would ease your mind, I would be happy to discuss the matter with you. Perhaps I may be of some help."

The judge thought to himself that this was a rather bold statement for such a young woman to make. He certainly was not in the habit of confiding in young women matters that related to his official duties. On the other hand, he enjoyed the company of Miss Tao and she was quite intelligent. Perhaps she could throw some light on the difficult case. So, the judge summarized for her the evidence he and his assistants had collected to date. After considering these facts silently for a while, Miss Tao said:

"It seems possible to draw some conclusions from this evidence, Your Honor. Everyone who saw Loo Ming the day he was murdered were customers of his and therefore all those who last saw him were wealthy."

"Why is that?" asked the judge.

"None of the silk Loo sells is cheap, since it is all custom dyed."

Suddenly the judge realized who was responsible for the crime. As he expressed his thanks to Miss Tao for her help, he reflected on his pleasure in finding such wisdom in one so young.

1.   What is the first argument offered by Miss Tao?

Premises: _____

_____

_____

Conclusion: _____

_____

2.	Is her first argument valid? Yes __ No __	Support your answer with a Venn diagram.

3.	What is Miss Tao's second argument?

	Premises: _____

	_____

	_____

	_____

	Conclusion: _____

	_____

4.	Is her second argument valid? Yes __ No __	Support your answer with a Venn diagram.

Judge Dee and the Case of the Boxing Master

With a look of great sadness, the judge turned to his trusted adviser Sergeant Hoong and said, "I am quite distressed by this case of Master Lan."

"I understand your disquiet, Your Honor. Master Lan was not only a fine athlete, but a very good man. I know that you greatly respected him for teaching his students the spiritual as well as the physical side of the martial arts. His murder is a great loss to the whole district."

"I would feel much better if I could solve this crime," replied the judge. "Let's review the facts and see if we can make some headway toward a solution. First, we know that everyone at the inn recognized Lan when he entered, because they all knew him. Further, we know that it cannot be true that both the innkeeper and his wife brought Lan's dinner to his room, because at least one of them was in the common room at all times. But that does mean that at least one or the other of them could have been in Master Lan's room for some part of the evening. I think that we should summon the innkeeper and his wife to appear at tomorrow morning's session of the tribunal."

"That would be wise, Your Honor," said the sergeant.

1. How does the judge arrive at the conclusion that everyone at the inn recognized Master Lan?

    Premises: _____

    _____

    _____

    _____

2. What kind of argument is the judge using here and what is its form?

3.	Is the judge correct to draw this conclusion from these premises?

4.	The judge says that he knows that both the innkeeper and his wife brought Lan's dinner to him in his room, because at least one of them was in the common room all night. The judge has come to this conclusion by means of two parallel arguments. Can you figure out what they are?

5.	What kind of arguments are these and are they valid?

_____

6.	Assuming, as the judge does, that either the innkeeper or his wife brought Lan his dinner to his room, what is the argument by which the judge concludes that at last one of them was in Lan's room that night?

7.	What kind of argument is this? Is it valid?

_____

Student: _____

Judge Dee Clears an Innocent Man

Judge Dee announced:

"This testimony proves that Kuo Feng told the truth about his movements on the fifteenth and sixteenth, namely that he had been out of the city on those days. Clearly, if he had been out of the city on the day the murder occurred, he could not be guilty. The objection of the plaintiff that the murder could have occurred before the fifteenth (the coroner's report left this possibility open) can be met with the following argument. Anyone who murdered Kuo's wife would not have left the city for two days without concealing the body at least temporarily. All those currently suspected of the crime, including Kuo himself, were out of the city during that time. Therefore, none of these suspects committed the murder. Kuo Feng is free to go!"

The citizens who had crowded into the tribunal to see the trial marveled at the wisdom of their judge.

1.   What is the judge's first argument for Kuo Feng's innocence?

    Premises: _____

    _____

    _____

    Conclusion: _____

    _____

2.   What is the judge's second argument for Kuo Feng's innocence?

    Premises: _____

    _____

    _____

    Conclusion: _____

    _____

3.   Are the arguments valid? Why or why not?

Judge Dee Detects a Fallacy

The judge turned to his lieutenant Chiao Tai and said, "Well, then, Chiao why don't you give us your version of the crime?"

Flattered by the judge's request for his opinion, Chiao straightened himself and, lifting his head a little, said:

"I see the case this way, Your Honor. Either Mrs. Lang put the poison in the cup herself or her maid did it at her direction, because only Mrs. Lang and her maid had access to the tea cup. Either way Mrs. Lang is guilty of murder."

The judge smiled and said, "Chiao Tai, you are a fine swordsman and a loyal assistant, but you are not a very critical thinker. Your argument is valid, but it still does not help us solve the crime."

The chief scribe, who overheard this conversation, quietly nodded his head with approval of the judge's wisdom.

1.   What is the logical form of Chiao Tai's argument?

2.   Is the judge correct to say it is valid? Why or why not?

_____

_____

3.   Why did Judge Dee say that Chiao's argument does not solve the crime?

_____

_____

_____

Judge Dee and the Search for a Tea Merchant

Judge Dee, while visiting the impressive residence of his colleague Magistrate Lo in Chin-hwa, was presented with the following problem. "You must excuse my unworthy welcome," said Lo, "but we are searching for the tea-merchant Meng."

"I see," answered Dee, "this is why all the personnel of your tribunal as well as your whole household are gathered here in the main courtyard."

"Yes, Meng was brought here within the tribunal walls this morning by my men for questioning, but now he has disappeared. I fear that he has somehow found his way out of the tribunal grounds and is now lost in the city. This is a puzzle, however, because there are only two ways out of the tribunal: through the main gate or over the walls. But if Meng took either way of escape, he would have been seen. We know that he is indeed not on the grounds, because we have searched thoroughly and the only people here are those gathered before you."

Stroking his long beard thoughtfully, Judge Dee said, "I am sure that you are correct, Lo, that anyone leaving the grounds would be seen. Therefore, it cannot be that Meng has left and was not seen. Assume for a moment that he did. Then, given what you say, he would have been seen, but we know that he was not seen. So, Meng cannot have left and not be seen. This leaves only one possibility, that Meng is still among us."

1.   What is the traditional name for the sort of argument Judge Dee is using?

_____

2.   What is the logical form of his argument?

Judge Dee Solves the Case of the Abducted Woman

The judge wearily closed the morning session of the tribunal and went to his private office. There the chief scribe assisted him in removing his ceremonial robe of green brocade and his winged cap of black silk. After getting into a more comfortable house robe, the judge settled into his desk chair and gratefully accepted the steaming cup of tea the assistant scribe offered him. His tranquility was shattered as his lieutenant Chiao Tai burst into the room with the news that all three of the Yeh brothers were dead.

"We found their bodies behind the Temple of the City God, Your Honor," Chiao reported, "so that means that they could not have been at the Covered Market this morning."

"Yes," said the judge, "we can only conclude that none of the witnesses told the truth when they reported seeing them at the market."

"Does this mean that our investigation must begin all over again?" asked Chiao Tai.

"Well, we at least know that if the Yeh brothers died behind the Temple of the City God then they could not have been at the Covered Market this morning. Further, we know that if they were not at the Covered Market this morning then they could not have been involved in the crime. Clearly your discovery means that they are not involved in the crime."

Turning to the chief scribe, the judge ordered, "Bring me the file on Pan Feng." Opening the file box the judge read through his notes on his earlier interrogation of Pan Feng. Suddenly his face brightened and, looking up, he smiled at Chiao Tai and said, "I shall give the solution of the case at the afternoon session of the tribunal."

A few hours later the judge took his place behind the bench and looked over the crowded tribunal hall. He reflected that news of his solving the disappearance of Miss Laio had spread quickly through the town. He then opened the session and, after reading the roll, he filled out an official form with Pan Feng's name and handed it to the warden. When Pan Feng was brought before the bench the judge asked him, "Was Miss Laio your lover?" Pan Feng turned pale. He realized that the judge now knew of his secret affair with the young woman.

In a voice hardly audible he answered, "Yes."

The judge then announced, "I thereby condemn you for the abduction and murder of Miss Laio Tai-yung!" The constables led the dumbfounded Pan away and the judge closed the session.

Back in the judge's private office Chiao Tai asked, "How did you know that Pan was guilty?"

"My reasoning was simple," replied the judge. "We already knew that whoever abducted Miss Laio had to be someone who knew her personally. The only people in town who knew her were the Yeh brothers and Pan Feng. Further, we knew that only someone who had been in the Covered Market this morning could have abducted her. Your discovery of the murders of the Yeh brothers showed that only Pan could have been in the Covered Market at right time. Clearly, Pan is the guilty party."

Chiao Tai was struck with admiration for Judge Dee's wisdom.

1.	What is the argument which leads the judge to conclude that none of the witnesses had been telling the truth when they said that they had seen the Yeh brothers in the market?

2.	How does the judge know that the Yeh brothers were not involved in the crime?

3.	What is the argument the judge uses to conclude that Pan Feng is guilty?

4.	Has the judge made the right decision in condemning Pan Feng? Why or why not?

Appendix III: Self-Testing Exercises

Identify and analyze each of the following arguments. Use schematic representations and, if possible, Venn diagrams to determine validity. Identify each argument by its traditional name. Identify each fallacy with its traditional name and explain where and how the error is committed in the argument. (The answers to these exercises begin on page 209.)

1. Among all human pursuits, the pursuit of wisdom is more perfect, more noble, more useful, and more full of joy than any other. What is more perfect, noble, practical, and enjoyed ought to be sought. Thus, wisdom must be sought by all through their human nature.

2. The purpose of each thing is that which is intended by its author or mover. But the author and mover of all things is an intellect, as can be shown in a separate argument. Therefore, the purpose of everything that exists is intellectual.

3. If the Senate objects to Gaius' motion, they will not pass it. Clearly, no senator favors his proposal. Therefore, it will not pass.

4. Either the world is eternal or it began in time. It cannot have begun in time. Therefore, it is eternal.

5. Some women are very good mathematicians. You don't think so? Well, let's assume you're right and women just aren't good at that sort of thing. Then there would be no women who are mathematical physicists, because even to get into that field one has to have great mathematical skill. But, I know several myself who are quite respected by their fellow physicists. This clearly contradicts your contention that no women are good at math. It follows that at least some women are good at mathematics.

6. If there is motion, time must be a reality. But time is unreal. So, no motion exists.

7. Some objects are in motion and everything which is in motion must have been moved by something other than itself. Therefore, there is something which has been moved by something other than itself.

8. All bodies which cast a circular shadow must have a curved surface. The earth casts a circular shadow on the surface of the moon during an eclipse. Therefore, the earth has a curved surface.

9. If the earth casts a curved shadow on the moon during an eclipse, then it must have at least one curved surface. Observations of eclipses confirm that a curved shadow is cast by the earth on the moon's surface. Therefore, the earth has at least one curved surface.

10. Divine things are eternal, thus, divine things lack potency.

11. It is impossible that the governor is at Rome and that he is in the provinces at the same time. We know from this report that he is addressing the Senate (at Rome) at this very hour. Thus, he clearly is not in the provinces.

12. Whatever is moved is moved by some finite series of moved movers. Nothing that is moved by a finite series of moved movers occupies an infinitely old universe. Therefore, everything that moves exists in a universe that had a beginning.

13. This cell is clearly about to reproduce. Why do I think so? Well, let's assume that I am wrong and it isn't about to divide. Then, its genetic material would be uniformly distributed throughout its mass. But, as you can see, the genetic material is grouped into two distinct areas. Therefore, the cell is about to divide.

14. Whatever matter is, it is in potency. Therefore, God is not matter.

15. If it is raining, the grass is wet. It is raining. Therefore, the grass is wet.

16. If it is raining, the grass is wet. It is not raining. Therefore, the grass is not wet.

17. If it is raining, the grass is wet. The grass is not wet. Therefore, it is not raining.

18. If it is raining, the grass is wet. The grass is wet. Therefore, it is raining.

19. All happy persons are content. No miser is content. Therefore, no miser is happy.

20. The following also shows that God cannot be a body. For every body is potentially divisible. But God is not potentially divisible. Thus, it is not possible that God should be a body.

21. There are some wicked men with great wealth. All wicked men are miserable. Therefore, there are some miserable men with great wealth.

22. When Judge Dee asked Lin Fan's widow why her husband killed himself, she answered, "Your Excellency, my honorable husband knew that either the victim's family would take matters into their own hands or he would be brought before the Tribunal; in either case he would hang." The judge considered the woman's words thoughtfully for a few moments, scratching his side whiskers. He then dismissed the case, confident that justice had been done.

23. Everything is good, because everything has been created by God.

24. One of the things that we must believe of God is that he is perfect, indeed the most perfect thing. The reason is that everything that is imperfect must be preceded by something that is perfect. An example is the seed which presupposes the animal or plant which has produced it. Now, God is not preceded by something which is perfect. Therefore, God cannot be imperfect.

25. If Patty was home, she would have let the dog out; you know she always does. So, if Patty was home you would be looking at the dog in the yard right now. But, as you can see, it's not there. Consequently, Patty cannot be home yet.

26. Some fools speak the truth. Whoever speaks the truth deserves to be imitated. Therefore, there are those who deserve to be imitated even though they are fools.

27. All good arguments for the existence of God are cosmological arguments. All cosmological arguments are based on invalid physics. Therefore, all good arguments for the existence of God are based on invalid physics.

28.	Every known physical body on earth or in the solar system regardless of size and composition is a physical body that obeys uniform laws of motion tending to a center of gravity in a local region. All planets are physical bodies. Thus, all planets obey uniform laws of motion tending to a center of gravity in a local region.

29.	Either this test material is defective or the substance is acid. We checked so we know that the test material is not defective. So, the substance is acid.

30.	All elements are the most basic parts of bodies with specific gravities and stable existences. All bodies with specific gravities and stable existences have weights in inverse relation to their distance from a center of gravity. Therefore, no elements have weights in inverse relation to their distance from a center of gravity.

31.	Every human society is grounded on a social contract. Some societies grounded on a social contract are not just. Therefore, some human societies are not just.

32.	If every disturbance in a medium is detectable, then it is measurable. Not every disturbance in a medium, however, is detectable. Thus, not every disturbance in a medium is measurable.

33.	Blood is a fluid of limited quantity that flows continuously in one direction. Thus, it circulates.

34.	If Newton had rejected the cosmological argument for the existence of God, he would have said so. But he didn't say so. Therefore, he did not reject the argument.

35.	An inert gas is an element with a neutral valance. Thus, inert gasses are chemically inactive.

36.	If something undergoes a radioactive transformation, it will tend to a stable nuclear structure. This can only happen if it releases energy. This can be proved if we assume that it does not release energy. If it does not release energy it is already stable, but we already showed that it was not yet stable if it is undergoing radioactive transformation. Therefore, the assumption that it isn't releasing energy cannot be true.

37. Every disturbance in a medium is detectable. Every disturbance in a medium is measurable. Therefore, everything detectable is measurable.

38. Stars are further away from the earth than planets. To prove this, assume that they are not. If that is true, then stars would emit steady light as the planets do. But the stars emit pulsating light (twinkle). Therefore, stars are further away than the planets.

39. Observe Watson! If Smythe told the truth then Miss Hanson committed the foul deed and Browne is lying. But either the Hanson woman didn't commit the murder or Browne isn't lying. Therefore, Smythe did not tell the truth.

40. Either everything is simple or life is too difficult to live. Nothing is simple in this life. Therefore, life is too difficult.

41. If I take the train, I will arrive in New York at 6:35. But if I take the plane, even though travel time will be much less, it will still take me until 6:35 to get into New York from the airport. The only two options open to me are train or plane. Thus, I will not get to New York until 6:35.

42. All members of the House of Lords have perfect self-command and nobody with perfect self-command should ride in a donkey race. Clearly, no member of the House of Lords should ride in a donkey race. Because this is true and any member of Parliament who is not a member of the House of Commons is a member of the House of Lords, it follows that all who should ride in a donkey race are members of the House of Commons. All members of the House of Commons also have perfect self-command. We are forced to conclude that everybody who rides in a donkey race should have perfect self-command.

43. If air has weight, then it exerts pressures which decrease as altitudes increase. If air exerts pressures which decrease as altitudes increase, then, this will be indicated on a Torricelli barometer. Thus, if air has weight, then this will be indicated on a Torricelli barometer.

44. When Diana marries Bill, Paul will be upset. When Paul is upset, he is difficult to live with. Therefore, when Diana marries Bill, Paul will be difficult to live with.

45. Any sodium salt, when put into the flame of a Bunsen burner, turns the flame yellow. Thus, rock salt will turn the flame yellow.

46.   One way in which some Arabic philosophers have argued to the eternity of the world is through the nature of efficient cause. Every effect, they point out, is produced through the power of God's efficiency. But God's efficiency is always eternal (for otherwise there would be potentiality in God). Therefore, every effect is eternal.

--adapted from St. Thomas Aquinas
Summa contra gentiles, II

47.   Either man is composed of body and soul or, as Plato thought, man is only soul using body, as Peter is not a thing composed of man and clothes, but a man using clothes. But Plato's opinion is impossible, because man could not, then, be a sensible thing. Therefore, man must be composed of body and soul.

--adapted from St. Thomas Aquinas
Summa contra gentiles, II

48.   From the fact that God is intelligent it follows that his act of understanding is his essence. This is because everything that is in God is his essence. Understanding is something that is in God and, so, understanding is his essence.

--adapted from St. Thomas Aquinas
Summa contra gentiles, I

49.   The knowledge of God would not be true and perfect unless things actually happen as God foresees. But God's knowledge is true and perfect (because he knows things as their creator). It follows that God foresees what will happen.

--adapted from St. Thomas Aquinas
Summa contra gentiles, I

50.   Only man is rational.
No woman is a man.
Therefore, no woman is rational.

51.   Since exercise is healthful, everyone with a heart condition should exercise every day.

52.   My former husband treated me badly. I have no doubt that all men would do the same and that is why I will never marry again.

53. Mr. Hobbes: People cannot help doing what they do in fact do.
     Mr. Arnold: Why not?
     Mr. Hobbes: Because they always follow the strongest motive they experience.
     Mr. Arnold: What, then, is their strongest motive?
     Mr. Hobbes: It is clearly the one they in fact follow.

54. Mr. Hume: It is not a crime to divert the Nile or the Danube from its course, if I can
                 do so.
     Mr. Kant: Indeed not. But what has this to do with the correctness of suicide?
     Mr. Hume: Well this: just as it is no crime to divert a river from its course, so it is no
                 crime to divert my blood from its course in my arteries. Thus, suicide is
                 not a crime.

55. Mr. Bacon: No body can be healthful without exercise and discipline.
     Mrs. Veil: I agree.
     Mr. Bacon: The same is true for the body politic (by which I mean the state). It cannot
                 be healthy without the exercise and discipline of honorable war.
     Mrs. Veil: This is why you think that war is good for the state?
     Mr. Bacon: Indeed it is, my good lady.

56. More young people attend high school and college today than ever before. But more
     young people are members of gangs today than ever before. Clearly, attending school is
     bad for young people.

57. Twist: Sir, this soup is cold.
     Bumbly: Cold! I suppose you want it scalding hot!
     Twist: No sir.
     Bumbly: Well, then, count yourself blessed--you didn't want it scalding and you
               didn't get it scalding.

58. Mr. Hume: The moral judgment that murder is wrong is based only on a personal
                 feeling of disgust.
     Mr. Aquino: How, then, do you explain that almost every human being makes this
                  judgment?
     Mr. Hume: The feeling of disgust of murderous acts is universal because all humans
                  feel it.

59. Either Socrates supports us or he is opposed to us.

60.   Bill: Diana, please call the Whitney Museum and ask if I can photograph some of the paintings in their exhibit.

Diana [over the phone]: Is picture-taking permitted at the exhibit today?

Museum Receptionist: No Madam, the pictures must be viewed hanging on the wall and cannot be removed.

61.   Dr. Large: You must go on a strict diet for the sake of your health.

Mrs. Magna: What do you know? You look as if you could use piece of your own advice! Clearly, you don't know what you are talking about.

Answers to Self-Testing Exercises

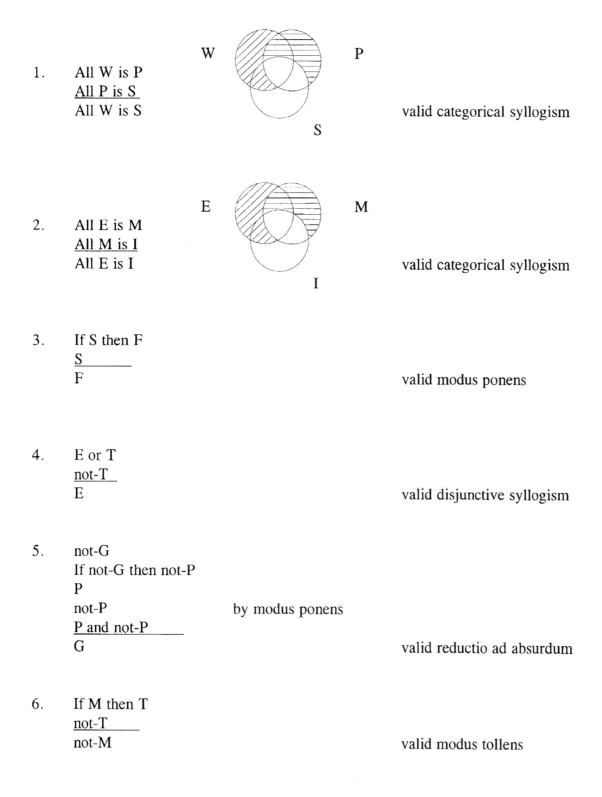

1. All W is P
    <u>All P is S</u>
    All W is S
                                        valid categorical syllogism

2. All E is M
    <u>All M is I</u>
    All E is I
                                        valid categorical syllogism

3. If S then F
    <u>S   </u>
    F
                                        valid modus ponens

4. E or T
    <u>not-T </u>
    E
                                        valid disjunctive syllogism

5. not-G
    If not-G then not-P
    P
    not-P   by modus ponens
    <u>P and not-P   </u>
    G
                                        valid reductio ad absurdum

6. If M then T
    <u>not-T   </u>
    not-M
                                        valid modus tollens

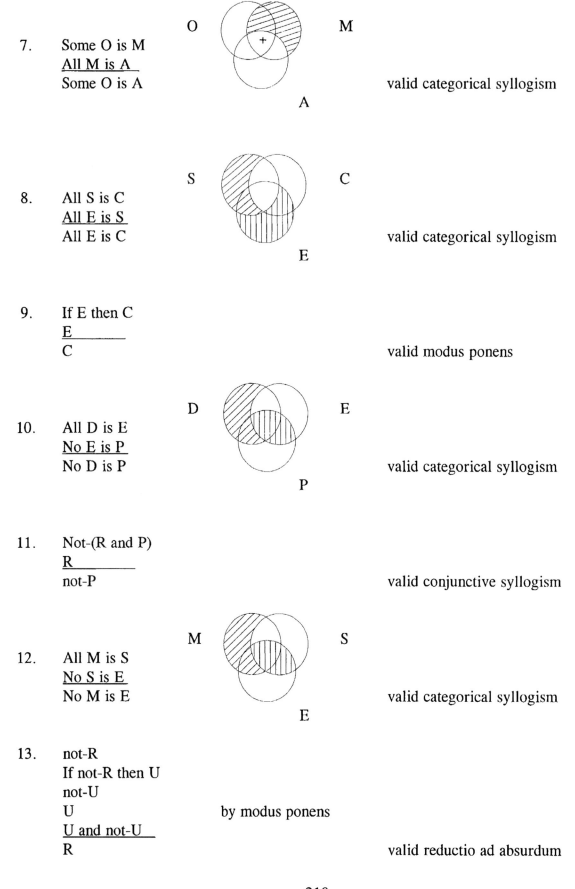

7.   Some O is M
       <u>All M is A</u>
       Some O is A   valid categorical syllogism

8.   All S is C
       <u>All E is S</u>
       All E is C   valid categorical syllogism

9.   If E then C
       <u>E</u>
       C   valid modus ponens

10.   All D is E
       <u>No E is P</u>
       No D is P   valid categorical syllogism

11.   Not-(R and P)
       <u>R</u>
       not-P   valid conjunctive syllogism

12.   All M is S
       <u>No S is E</u>
       No M is E   valid categorical syllogism

13.   not-R
       If not-R then U
       not-U
       U   by modus ponens
       <u>U and not-U</u>
       R   valid reductio ad absurdum

14. All M is P
    No G is P
    No G is M

valid categorical syllogism

15. If R then W
    R
    W

valid modus ponens

16. If R then W
    not-R
    not-W

invalid denying the antecedent

17. If R then W
    not-W
    not-R

valid modus tollens

18. If R then W
    W
    R

invalid affirming the consequent

19. All H is C
    No M is C
    No M is H

valid categorical syllogism

20. All B is P
    No G is P
    No G is B

valid categorical syllogism

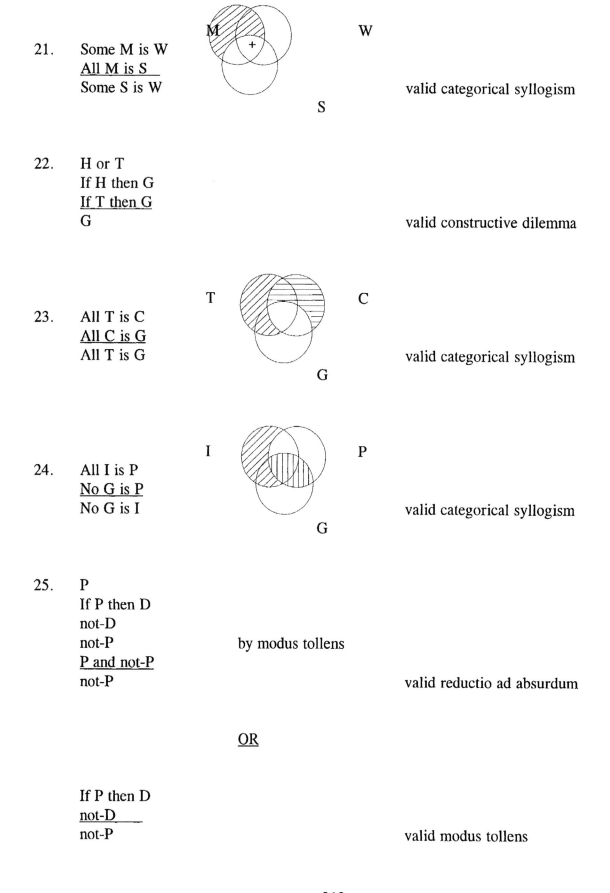

21. Some M is W
    All M is S
    Some S is W

    valid categorical syllogism

22. H or T
    If H then G
    If T then G
    G

    valid constructive dilemma

23. All T is C
    All C is G
    All T is G

    valid categorical syllogism

24. All I is P
    No G is P
    No G is I

    valid categorical syllogism

25. P
    If P then D
    not-D
    not-P   by modus tollens
    P and not-P
    not-P

    valid reductio ad absurdum

              OR

    If P then D
    not-D
    not-P

    valid modus tollens

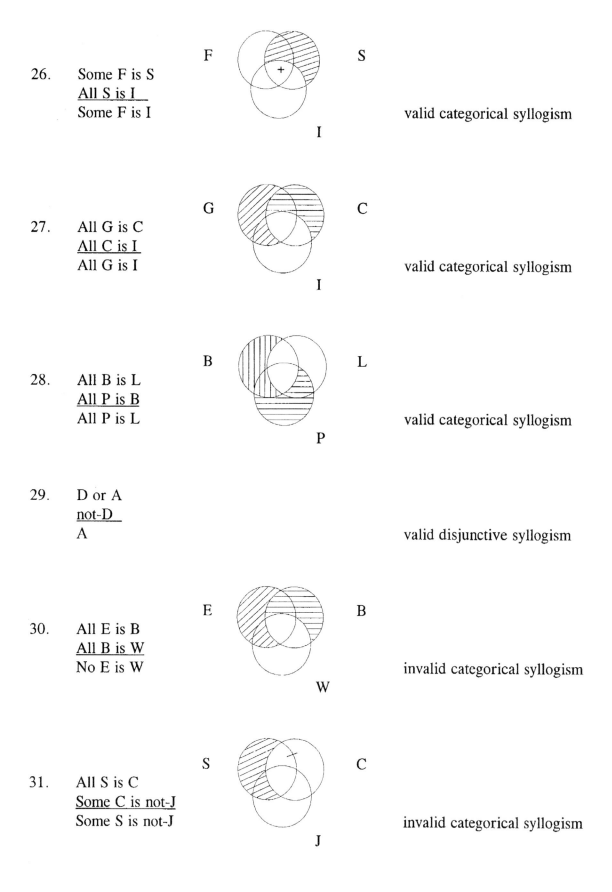

26. Some F is S
    <u>All S is I</u>
    Some F is I

    valid categorical syllogism

27. All G is C
    <u>All C is I</u>
    All G is I

    valid categorical syllogism

28. All B is L
    <u>All P is B</u>
    All P is L

    valid categorical syllogism

29. D or A
    <u>not-D</u>
    A

    valid disjunctive syllogism

30. All E is B
    <u>All B is W</u>
    No E is W

    invalid categorical syllogism

31. All S is C
    <u>Some C is not-J</u>
    Some S is not-J

    invalid categorical syllogism

32. If D then M
     <u>not-D</u>
     not-M   invalid denying the antecedent

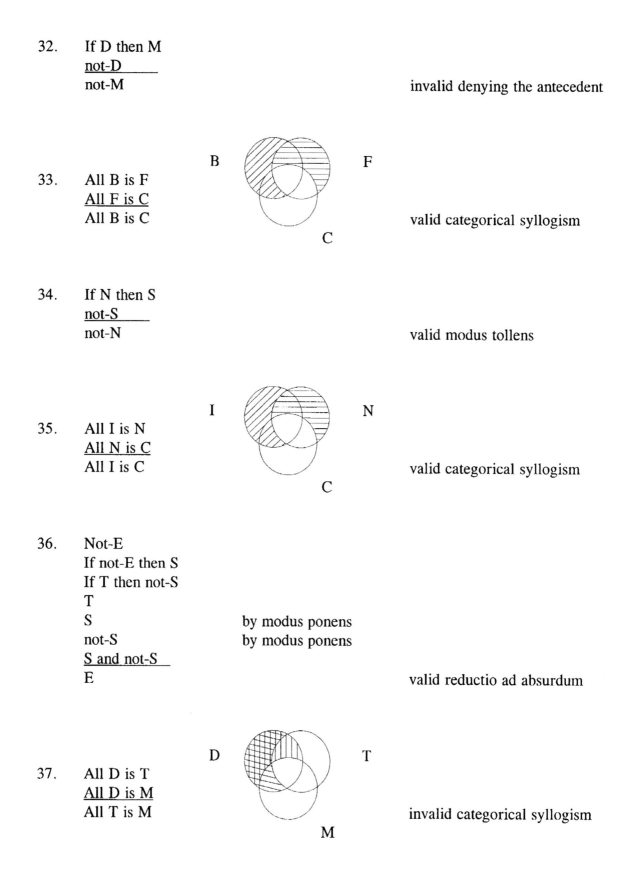

33. All B is F
     <u>All F is C</u>
     All B is C   valid categorical syllogism

34. If N then S
     <u>not-S</u>
     not-N   valid modus tollens

35. All I is N
     <u>All N is C</u>
     All I is C   valid categorical syllogism

36. Not-E
     If not-E then S
     If T then not-S
     T
     S   by modus ponens
     not-S   by modus ponens
     <u>S and not-S</u>
     E   valid reductio ad absurdum

37. All D is T
     <u>All D is M</u>
     All T is M   invalid categorical syllogism

38. not-F
    If not-F then S
    not-S
    S   by modus ponens
    S and not-S
    F   valid reductio ad absurdum

39. If S then H
    If S then B
    not-H or not-B
    not-S   valid destructive dilemma

40. S or D
    not-S
    D   valid disjunctive syllogism

41. If T then A
    If P then A
    T or P
    A   valid constructive dilemma

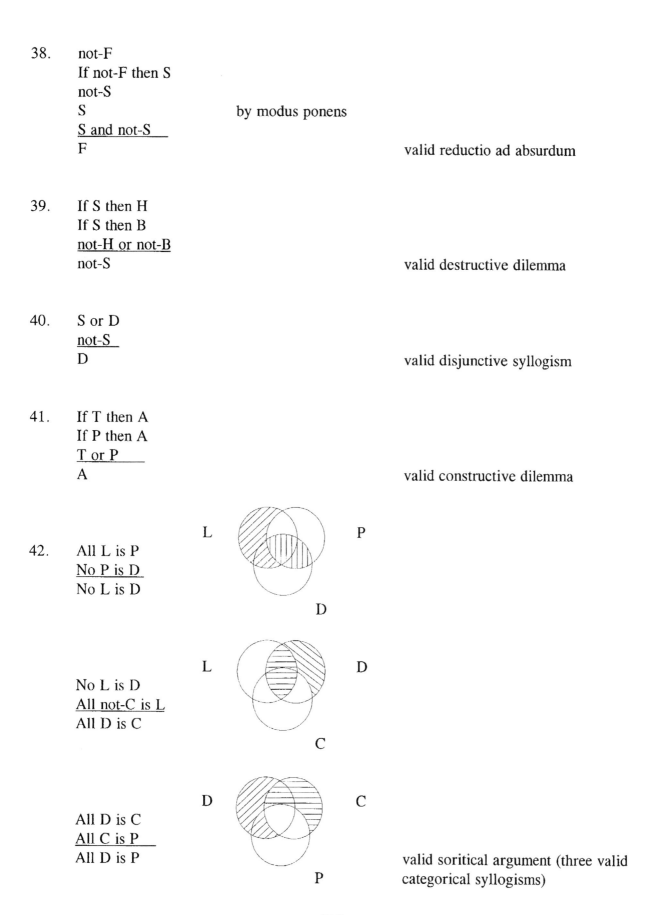

42. All L is P
    No P is D
    No L is D

    No L is D
    All not-C is L
    All D is C

    All D is C
    All C is P
    All D is P   valid soritical argument (three valid
                                               categorical syllogisms)

43. If W then P
If P then B
If W then B

valid hypothetical syllogism

44. If D then P
If P then L
If D then L

valid hypothetical syllogism

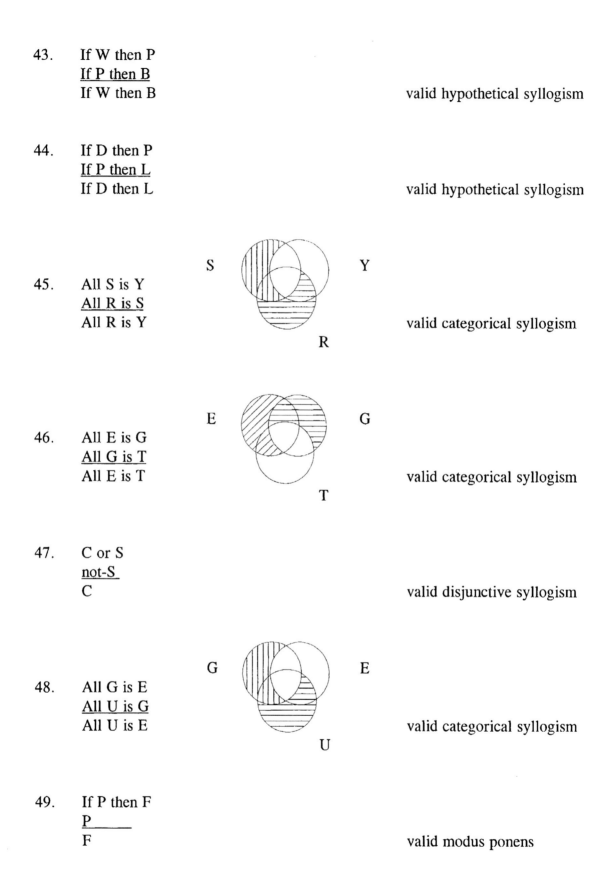

45. All S is Y
All R is S
All R is Y

valid categorical syllogism

46. All E is G
All G is T
All E is T

valid categorical syllogism

47. C or S
not-S
C

valid disjunctive syllogism

48. All G is E
All U is G
All U is E

valid categorical syllogism

49. If P then F
P
F

valid modus ponens

50.   Equivocation on the word "man." In the first premise "man" is being used generically and means "human being." In the second premise "man" is being used specifically and means "male." This argument, then, has four not three terms and therefore is not a true categorical syllogism.

51.   Sweeping Generalization. In general it is true that exercise is good for your health. But there are exceptional cases, such as certain kinds of illness, where this general rule does not apply. This is the case here.

52.   Hasty Generalization. Just because one man acted in a certain way does not mean that all men will act in that way. Thus, the one case cited as evidence is not enough to prove the general rule true.

53.   Begging the Question. Mr. Hobbes tries to argue that the reason it must be true that people must do what they do in fact do is that they always follow their strongest motive. But it turns out that this reason is true only if his conclusion is true, namely, that people must do what they do. He is arguing in a circle.

54.   False Analogy. Mr. Hume compares diverting a river from its natural course and diverting blood from its natural course. But the issue here is a moral one and it is just in this respect that the two cases are different.

55.   False Analogy. While it may be possible to claim that a state and a human body are alike in some ways, these are of course very different in other ways. Exercise is good for the human body, but does this sort of activity really apply to an abstract thing such as a state?

56.   False Cause. The arguer here is trying to make a causal claim, but the only evidence he has is that the two events are going on at the same time. This is not enough to prove that the two are related as cause and effect.

57.   False Dichotomy. Mr. Bumbly is acting as though Twist has only two choices: cold soup or scalding hot soup. But, of course, there is really another possibility: warm soup and this is what Twist is requesting.

58.   Begging the Question. Mr. Hume assumes what he is trying to prove. To say that all humans feel the disgust is the same thing as saying that the feeling of disgust is universal.

59.   False Dichotomy. This disjunction seems to say that the only possibilities are Socrates supporting us or Socrates opposing us. But, of course, it is logically possible that Socrates neither supports us nor is opposed to us. Perhaps Socrates has no opinion on the issue between us.

60.   Equivocation on the term "picture-taking." Diana, of course, is talking of photographing while the Museum Receptionist thinks that she means taking the pictures off the wall!

61.   Tu quoque. Even if it is true that Dr. Large needs to go on a diet too, that does not prove that he is wrong that Mrs. Magna should diet. The doctor's advice might be good even if he does not follow it himself.